IRON in *SILK*

IRON in *SILK*

Miskyah

IRON in *SILK*

First edition 2023
Miskyah.com
Tierboskloof
Hout Bay
South Africa
7806

Text © Miskyah, 2023
First edition © Miskyah, 2023

All rights reserved

No part of this work may be reproduced or stored in any retrieval system, whether electronic or mechanical, by photocopying, recording, or otherwise, without the written permission of the publisher. If it is planned to use any part of this work for educational purposes, prior permission must be obtained from the publisher. Various names, characters, places, and incidents are the product of the author's memory. Some names and identifying details have been changed to protect the privacy of individuals.

Editor and proofreader: Ilana van Wyk
Cover design by Jason Mally
Typed in 13 pt on 16 pt Adobe Garamond Pro
First edition: Miskyah.com, October 2023
Printed and bound by Print on Demand, Cape Town
ISBN (Hardcover Printed): 978-1-991256-55-3
ISBN: (E-book): 978-991256-56-0

DEDICATION

I dedicate this book to my sons, Dean and Michael. Since you were babies, you were always my greatest inspiration to never quit. Today, just looking at your phenomenal lives and your wisdom, success, and humility is enough to inspire me to the greatest heights ever. I love you dearly.

ACKNOWLEDGEMENTS

First and foremost, I thank my heavenly Father for loving and keeping me so that this book could see the light. He prepared many tables for me in the presence of my enemies, but also for those I love. Enough for me to know that none of my enemies were ever flesh and blood… Some tables served bread only while others serve six-course meals, which take longer to get through, yet delight every form of appetite.

To everyone mentioned in this autobiography, thank you for the role you played in my life. All of it shaped me into the woman I am today. I've learned long ago that swift forgiveness and unconditional love is not easy, but not negotiable for success.

Thank you to my lovely Business Directive Contract Services (Pty) Ltd support team as well as the encouragement of committed friends and family. You gave me the boldness to become vulnerable enough to write about the challenges I faced in my life. If these didn't become stepping stones, how would I ever encourage anyone to become greater than their past? My soul is in iron, and I hope the silk you see, is a call to your heart to never let anything hold you back on your journey through life.

PROLOGUE

Life is precarious. Uncertainty about our future is a fact of life. As children, we all get lost in our daydreams. Our daydreams know no limitations or boundaries. Like an Eagle, we soar above any obstacles. In our daydreams, we are the hero of our own story. There is nothing we can't do. THEN LIFE HAPPENS.

As a child, my mind was set on becoming an entrepreneur. In my mind, I was the owner of my own business. Being born just at the end of the Baby Boomers era and their way of thinking conflicted with my daydreams. Economists define Baby Boomers as people born between 1946 to 1964. I was born in 1965. A tidal wave of births created the appropriately named Baby Boomer generation, as they represent a boom in the birth rate. The typical dream of this era was to have a large family, a steady job, and a house in the suburbs with a white picket fence. The norm was to study and get a good permanent job somewhere where you work until you retire. Changing jobs branded you as someone who cannot be trusted.

I was raised by conservative parents and originally followed the Baby Boomer trend as you will learn in my story. However, my childhood daydreams stuck with me like a stubborn knapsack that sticks to one's clothes or stockings. The typical Baby Boomer path of life created an emptiness inside of me. That feeling of in-betweenness as though you are en route to somewhere else. Most of us probably experience this during our lifetime. Many do not act on it, especially not to move from a life of certainty to a life of uncertainty that entrepreneurs experience. That is why less than 4% of the world's population are entrepreneurs.

Our childhood dream is the root of our soul. I could no longer ignore my innate talents and passion by allowing the societal norms of right and wrong to hold me back. It was not an easy decision and I certainly learned that successful entrepreneurship is a precarious journey. Making it in the world of entrepreneurship is exhilarating, intense, challenging, sometimes scary, and certainly requires a lot of hard and smart work.

Let us fast forward to years later when I met André Diederichs in Gordon's Bay in the Western Cape, South Africa. André consulted many businesses in his lifetime and still manages the Family Business Association of Southern Africa. It was during this time that I experienced many challenges in my personal and business life. I was a mother of two boys who also had to keep the pot boiling through my business. It has always been important to me to teach my boys that a woman does not have to sacrifice her femininity in the world of business. She can be a nurturer but also a warrior in the same manner the Bible describes the woman of valour in Proverbs 31.

André has an inquisitive mind and it was not long before I shared my journey as an entrepreneur and mother with him. We became friends over time as my business interests began to grow excessively. One day he intently looked at me. I could see he was deep in thought and waited to hear what he wanted to say to me. When he finally spoke, he said: "I must introduce you as a speaker at our next presentation to business people. I don't just want to tell the audience about your business successes. No, I want to try to explain to them who you are."

He remained quiet for a moment and then continued: "You manage your business interests with an iron grip but at the same time, you are someone who exudes femininity. It's a rare combination. If I had to sum you up in a title for a book the title would be, Iron in Silk."

I was intrigued by his description and asked. "I suppose the silk represents my femininity and the iron is like the expression, nerves of steel?"

"Yes. They called Margaret Thatcher, who served as Prime Minister of the United Kingdom, the Iron Lady. The way you deal with business reminds me of her. Silk to me is feminine but also indicates patience. I read somewhere that silkworms have played a significant role in shaping cultures throughout Europe and Asia. Silk production has been practised for over 5,000 years in China and Europe as early as the 6th century AD. Silk was, still is, and will always be a priceless treasure for many women. Chinese proverbs and the Bible, teach us the power of patience. The Chinese said that with time and patience, the mulberry leaf becomes a silk gown. Have you heard about the businesswoman Lydia in the Bible?"

I eagerly reacted: "Yes, I believe she was the most successful businesswoman in Biblical times."

"Yes. She was a wealthy and influential businesswoman who controlled the purple trade. A prized colour made from certain snails. Purple was a symbol of prestige. In the Bible, priests and royalty, including King David and King

Solomon, are often described as wearing clothing dyed with this colour. Like silk, it took patience to produce this colour. I believe that you are today reaping major benefits as a woman in business and a mother because of your patience over the years. Your life is similar to that of Lydia. You both understand the power of patience which I believe is only possible through faith and trust. You are proof of the words of wisdom that state that if you are patient in one moment of anger, you will escape a hundred days of sorrow."

The insights André shared with me had a significant impact on me and further encouraged me to change my daydreams as a child into reality. I invite you to experience my life story and experience how patience, faith and trust can help you to become content with your life.

ONE

22 September 2023.

Today is my birthday. Fifty-eight years ago, I bravely escaped from the safeness of my mother's womb to meet the world. I was born in Sasolburg in the far north of the Free State province of South Africa on 22 September 1965. I share my birthday with Andrea Bocelli, the Italian singer-songwriter and Princess Märtha Louise of Norway.

I found some fun facts on Google. 22 September, 1965, was a Wednesday and it was the 265th day of the year. The next time you can reuse your old 1965 calendar will be in 2027. Both calendars will be exactly the same. That is only a few years from now! If you've been sleeping 8 hours daily since birth, then you have slept 7,060 days or 19.33 years. You spent 33% of your life sleeping. As an entrepreneur for most of my life, I certainly slept much less than 8 hours a day!

As a baby, I did not know what was going on in the world around me, but history gives you an idea. On my birthdate, the India and Pakistan cease-fire went into effect, ending the Indo-Pakistani War. In the same year, Sir Winston Churchill's funeral took place in London with the largest assembly of dignitaries in the world at that stage. Humankind's need to explore the unknown includes outer space. In that year the U.S. spacecraft Mariner 4 was the first spacecraft to fly by Mars, and the first to return close-up images of the Red Planet. Growing up in South

Africa, I experienced the effects of Apartheid. This struggle was also going on elsewhere in the world because in 1965 the Voting Rights Act, guaranteeing African Americans the right to vote, became law. In the same year, the African National Congress established its headquarters in Morogoro, Tanzania.

Let us return to Sasolburg where I was born. Apartheid had led to many sanctions against South Africa. It forced the government of the day to become entrepreneurial. They could not buy oil from other countries to produce fuel and had to find an alternative solution. South Africa is coal-rich and our scientists learned to process, or change, coal into liquid fuel. This was a first for the world, and many parts of the world hated this innovative spirit of South Africans. The South African government created Sasol to produce synthetic fuels. The town of Sasolburg was born in the year 1954 to provide adequate lodging for employees of Sasol and also as a base for other operational equipment for the company.

My father, Fanie Prinsloo, worked for Sasol, and that is why we lived there. My mother, Corrie, was a music teacher. Mother had a beautiful operatic soprano voice. The world-renowned South African soprano opera singer Mimi Coertse gave her singing lessons. Mother had a euphonious voice that could mesmerize you. When I was upset, her singing calmed my soul as though I was listening to the pure and beautiful sound of an angel.

My brothers were seven and four years older than me and did not take notice of their little sister. I had friends since my early childhood but my best friend was my daydreams. Since my childhood, I never seemed to bore myself. I kept to myself and made sure that I stayed out of trouble.

My fondest memories were of when we visited Uncle Hennie and Aunt Hetta during the school holidays. They had a holiday resort near Graskop in Mpumalanga province, in South Africa. Graskop started in the 1880s as a gold mining camp but became a very popular tourist destination. The nature is breathtaking there. They compare the natural wonders of Graskop with the best scenes in the world. God's Window boasts truly dramatic views into the indigenous forest. Its vegetation is both varied and lush, with a rich selection of bird life. Close by is the Blyde River Canyon. It is the third largest in the world and one of South Africa's popular scenic wonders.

Childhood is the time when most people dream about the future and let their imaginations soar. Many events can influence and change a child's fantasies over the years and even change their minds about what they want to become in the world. If you are a parent, you will know how many times your children change their minds about what they want to become or who they want to be. This is normal.

Sadly, when they grow up many people stop following their childhood dreams when reality bites. This is sad because daydreams transport you to your happy place. To stop dreaming turns life into a monotonous series of events.

No compass guides you on the path you have to follow to realise your dreams. I know this because it has taken me a long time to get there myself. Life leads us through unexpected detours and challenging obstacles before we fulfil our daydreams. Turning your daydreams into reality is not always a smooth path, but to just dream about your happy place and not act upon it will just remain a dream. You must add wings to your dream to fly towards your dream destination.

Today I know that those unknown paths I had to walk were part of preparing me to make my childhood dreams come true. It's as if the entrepreneurial spirit that brought Sasol into existence remained stuck somewhere in my spirit. I am extremely grateful that my childhood dreams did not stop in the face of the realities I had to deal with. The words in the Impossible Dream song by Roger Whittaker resonate with me because it encourages us to reach for the stars.

> To dream ... the impossible dream ...
> To fight ... the unbeatable foe ...
> To bear ... with unbearable sorrow ...
> To run ... where the brave dare not go ...
> To right ... the unrightable wrong ...
> To love ... pure and chaste from afar ...
> To try ... when your arms are too weary ...
> To reach ... the unreachable star ...
>
> This is my quest, to follow that star ...
> No matter how hopeless, no matter how far ...
> To fight for the right, without question or pause ...
> To be willing to march into Hell, for a Heavenly cause ...
>
> And I know if I'll only be true, to this glorious quest
> That my heart will lie peaceful and calm
> When I'm laid to my rest ...

And the world will be better for this:
That one man, scorned and covered with scars
Still strove, with his last ounce of courage
To reach ... the unreachable star ...
Let me return to my childhood to continue my journey down memory lane...

TWO

In my 2nd grade, I had to deal with actual change for the first time in my life. My father accepted a new position at Valindaba, also known as Pelindaba East or Y-plant, an experimental uranium enrichment plant. It is located 35 km west of Pretoria, in the Gauteng province of South Africa. South Africa is the world's tenth-largest producer of uranium.

Uranium is a contentious element. It has the highest atomic weight of all naturally occurring elements and is an essential part of nuclear warfare. South Africa was involved in the Border War, from 1966 to 1989. Communist countries like the old USSR backed this war against South Africa. The official purpose of the Pelindaba facility was to harness the versatile power of the atom for non-threatening purposes, such as nuclear power stations. However, by 1996, South Africa could produce atomic weapons. Valindaba is a Zulu word that means "about this, we do not speak at all." It is ironic that communism also crumbled in 1989, at the end of our Border war, with the fall of the Berlin Wall in Germany.

As a 2nd-grade pupil, I was not aware of the Border War or nuclear weapons. Our household had a fixed routine with no disturbances. In my limited world, the move from Sasolburg to Pretoria introduced me to the unknown. It was scary and exciting at the same time.

Our home was on Milton Avenue in Waverley. Waverley is a suburb in the city of Pretoria, South Africa. Located just northeast of the CBD in a leafy, established area that is home to some well-constructed residences on large stands. Its neighbouring suburbs are Rietfontein and Villieria.

I joined Totiusdal Primary School where I met my best friend, Elbie du Toit. My mother was the maths and music teacher at the school and was very strict with me. She did not put me forward because I was her daughter. She was stricter with me than the other children. I did well in school and became the head girl of my school.

My high school career began in 1979 at Oos Moot where I matriculated in 1983. Our school's motto was work and conquer. This motto became a reality in my personal life. In the 9th grade, my best friend Elbie and her family moved to another city, but we still keep in touch to this day.

Apart from my first kiss with Henk, nothing extraordinary happened to me in my high school career. Henk was from Queenswood. A gentle boy who treated me with great respect. Henk tried valiantly to keep me but lost the battle when in my final year at school, I met George, who turned my peaceful existence on its head. Because of the age difference, my parents were continuously watching that he didn't act inappropriately.

After matric, I went to study social sciences at the University of Pretoria. It was not my first choice, but it was in line with the typical thinking of that time. The plan was to complete my degree and become a teacher like my mom. It was more my parents' choice than my own. My dream of entering the business world was still as alive in my mind as it had been as a young child.

My father resigned from Valindaba in my third year to

pursue his lifelong dream of farming, as he did before he moved to Sasolburg. The farm was between Lydenburg and Ohrigstad. Lydenburg is a town in the Mpumalanga Highveld, in South Africa. It is situated in the foothills of the famous Long Tom Pass and surrounded by the Steenkampsberg and Mauchsberg mountain ranges. My father started farming there with cattle and sheep and also started a dairy.

George did not let the grass grow under his feet and we were married in 1986, during my third year. We had a house built in The Reeds at Centurion and moved there.

I also got bored with my studies in my third year. I studied part-time and got a job at OK Bazaars as a training human resource manager. OK Bazaars is one of the oldest retail shops in South Africa. Partners Michael Miller and Sam Cohen established it in 1927. The first shop opened on the corner of President and Eloff streets in Johannesburg. It expanded all over the country and is still in existence today.

This was my first baby step into the world of business and I applied the motto of my school, to work hard and conquer, with total dedication. I progressed quickly in my career at OK Bazaars. They appointed me as the Human Resources manager at the Wespark branch just a month later.

I had barely started there when I had to face a six-week strike. Violence accompanied it, and I had to learn how to defuse the situation. As an inexperienced girl, it felt to me like I had to swim with the sharks. It was nerve-wracking and exhilarating at the same time. This experience prepared me for the challenges that the business world faces.

I quickly learned that nothing stays static in the business world. There are constant changes. Just as a whirlpool is ever-rotating, there are constant changes in the competitive marketplace. Should you fall into a whirlpool, the only way to survive is to swim with the current. If you swim against the current, you will probably drown. Make sure you understand essential changes and adapt to them. If not, you will drown in the business world, just as someone who tries to swim against the current will drown.

Life can throw you many curveballs in your personal life and business. We may experience curveballs or defeats, but must not let them defeat us. Curve balls offer us lessons in life and business. Lessons have a peculiar way of repeating themselves if you do not learn from the lesson and change what you should change. Dealing with curve balls is part of learning and growing as a person. It teaches you about yourself and what you can rise from to find your highest potential self. Let me share the curveballs I had to deal with, with you and also how I learned to hit them out of the park!

THREE

Birth and death are an experience that every person goes through. It marks the beginning and end of our physical existence. Recognising the inevitability of death can serve as a reminder of the preciousness of life. It emphasises the significance of the time we have on this earth and suggests that our actions and choices during our lifetime truly matter.

A poem by Linda Ellis reveals a simple truth. "I read of a man who stood to speak at the funeral of a friend. He referred to the dates on the tombstone from the beginning...to the end. For that dash represents all the time that they spent alive on earth. And now only those who loved them know what that brief line is worth..." God controls when we are born and die. What we do in the dash between birth and death is significant.

In a normal lifespan, we all experience major events, along with countless smaller ones. Collectively, these events shape our journey through life and contribute to our story. To me, marriage and the birth of a child are major events that come without a manual. We learn through trial and error.

Marriage can be challenging and rewarding. Each person brings their own set of expectations and beliefs into a marriage. The impact of different backgrounds can be significant and multifaceted. When individuals from diverse backgrounds come together, it presents challenges. These differences can have both positive and challenging effects on the relationship.

A fulfilling career can have both positive and challenging effects on your marriage and parenthood. My daydream of owning my business did not stop because I got married and became a mother.

My upbringing led to a Calvinistic approach to my marriage. My approach to business was, and still is, daring, but my approach to marriage is conservative. Calvinism is a branch of Protestant Christianity founded by John Calvin in the 16th century. It has a significant influence on various aspects of life, including marriage. Calvinism doesn't have a distinct set of marriage rituals or rules. However, it offers certain theological and moral principles that can shape the approach to marriage for adherents.

Calvinistic views on marriage are often based on biblical teachings about marriage. We know Calvinism for its covenant theology, which views God's relationship with His people as a series of covenants. Marriage, according to this perspective, is a covenant between a husband, a wife, and God. This covenant is to be taken seriously and intends to reflect the covenant relationship between Christ and the Church.

Dean, my first child, was born in April 1989 after three years of marriage. I experienced overwhelming joy and happiness when I first saw and held Dean in my arms. The sense of wonder and amazement at this new life that I've brought into the world was to be truly uplifting. The love I felt for him was immediate and unconditional. It's a profound love that is unlike any other love one can experience.

Alongside the joy and love I felt, there were feelings of

nervousness and anxiety. As a new mother, I worried about my ability to care for and protect this precious gift of life. It overwhelmed me. I left my job at OK Bazaars to attend to his needs.

George was equally excited about the birth of Dean, but something between us changed. My female intuition probably made me feel that his loyalty to Dean didn't include me. It felt as though I became only a means to an end and that his marriage vows to me waned. My intuition had not betrayed me. George explored new pastures, and it was the beginning of the end of our marriage.

My Calvinistic faith emphasises the importance of commitment and fidelity in marriage. I believe that what God joins may not be separated. Divorce is a last resort and discouraged, except in cases of adultery or abandonment, which are biblically accepted grounds for divorce.

The end of a significant relationship like marriage is emotionally overwhelming and raises many questions in our minds. As a woman, you question yourself and wonder what you did to deserve this. It triggers a rollercoaster of emotions, including sadness, grief, anger, anxiety, and feelings of loss. However, I could not stay with someone who was not completely faithful to me and in 1990, we got divorced.

The divorce led to the next battle in my life. The battle for children during a divorce can be emotionally challenging and legally complex. Material things and children are normally at the centre of this battle. George wanted custody of Dean. The words, "You should never come between a mother and her child," became a reality and triggered the warrior within me. I had a disadvantage because I did not have a proper job at that stage, but I could easily rectify that.

To settle the argument as quickly as possible, I left almost all our assets to George. It was easy to find a job at a recruitment agency because they paid commission only. We moved to Randburg in Johannesburg for this job. The agency paid me a healthy 45% commission. This was my first step into self-employment because they only paid me for the new business I brought to the agency.

The phrase: "people under pressure can do wonders," suggests that individuals can achieve remarkable things when they face challenging situations. I was adamant to be financially independent. Facing this pressure boosted my resilience and success fed my self-confidence. It is amazing how success in such a high-pressure situation can boost an individual's belief in their abilities. I learned how success can create a virtuous cycle because success breeds more success.

The agency underestimated my abilities and offered me a partnership to rid themselves of the high commission I earned. They offered me a fixed salary with a much lower commission. I accepted the offer because I thought it would be a more secure income for us. This was my first genuine mistake in my business life because I did not receive the promised salary and had to leave the job within two months. The most important lesson I learned was that I should never totally entrust my future to other people.

I ended up in Melville in Johannesburg with my baby, with no financial backup. I could not rely on my parents. My father's injury on the farm forced him to sell the farm. They went through their own financial struggles. It forced me to ask George and his new wife to help us. This was very difficult but in the interest of my baby. Approaching someone with whom you share a sad history can be intimidating. You fear they will reject your request or use it as an opportunity to humiliate you. To be honest, asking George for financial help was a blow to my pride and self-respect. However, the welfare of my son was my highest priority and I had to swallow this bitter pill.

My biggest fear was that asking George for support would come with strings attached, such as expectations to give my custody of Dean over to him. He offered to take care of Dean until I found my feet again. I was adamant about making this happen soon and ended up doing three jobs to regain my financial stability. I started teaching at a Christian school, did telesales and did administrative jobs for various people.

In 1991, I started working at a recruitment company again. My boss, Jannie, knew I was a teacher at a Christian School. He told me to not speak about Christianity in the workplace. It did not bother me much since I believed in God and lived according to Biblical principles but was not a fully converted Christian. At that stage of my life, my faith in myself overshadowed my faith or total dependency on God. However, my ethical approach to my work must have rubbed off on him. This became apparent when he unexpectedly remarked: "Working with you convinced me to never again appoint someone who is not a Christian."

Later in 1991, my fear came true when George wouldn't give Dean back to me. It made me rebellious and despondent at the same time. This brought me to a place in my life where I sought deeper answers about the purpose of all the struggles in my life.

I felt emotionally drained and turned to Radio Pulpit, a Christian radio station, to seek spiritual upliftment. I listened to Rev. Johann Els' talk. He spoke about the radical conversion of Saul of the Bible on the road to Damascus. His words deeply touched my spirit and at that moment I knew that my life resonated with the life of Saul on the road to Damascus. I also needed a radical change in my life. I started praying for forgiveness and completely surrendered my life to Jesus Christ, our Lord and Saviour.

It's important to note that the experience of a conversion to Jesus Christ can vary among individuals. Some may experience a sudden and dramatic transformation, while others may go through a more gradual process of coming to faith. My conversation was like that of Saul. I completely and permanently converted to Christ. It was a profound and transformative experience in which I fully placed my trust in Jesus and not in my abilities anymore. Saul changed his name to Paul. Saul means big man and Paul means a small man. This is significant because Saul had to become less to allow Jesus to take over the reins of his life. This type of conversion involves a deep spiritual awakening. I also handed the reins of my life over to Him and have followed His guidance for my life from that day onwards.

Bruce Wilkinson's book, Secrets of the Vine, helped me to understand what happened to me. The book deals with John 15 in the Bible, where Jesus stated: "I am the True Vine, and My Father is the Vinedresser." It taught me that God cares more about my soul than anything else. God will allow drama into my life if I don't want to listen, and will deepen that drama until I listen. It is like the vine that is pruned. The deeper we prune it, the more fruit it will bear. He wants us to bear more fruit and will cut us where it hurts if we don't want to hear. My biggest pain was the separation between my child and myself. I had to give Him control of my life before He intervened to remove the pain.

Profound events affect the way we see life. It defines our purpose. We experience highs and lows and unexpected events on our journey through life. It reveals who we are and how we deal with adversity. Let this journey continue…

FOUR

The year 1992 brought challenges and surprises. I experienced communal living in Northcliff. I shared the house with other women. Co-housing arrangements can save you money. We shared chores, enjoyed group activities, and formed lasting friendships. We all had our own private lives and our individual living spaces. However, we shared a garden, a laundry room, and a kitchen.

What we wish we did not have to share, was our fear of the Norwood serial killer. Kobus Geldenhuys–the Norwood Serial Killer–was South Africa's equivalent of the narcissist Ted Bundy. Geldenhuys, who was a police officer, carried out his crimes in the suburb of Norwood in Johannesburg between 1991 and 1992.

The newspapers wrote: "Geldenhuys's more serious crimes bear some eerie resemblances to those of Bundy. Both broke into women's homes to commit brutal rapes and murder. They both planned their attacks carefully and patiently and had a superior disregard for authority. They showed no empathy or remorse." In 1993, they sentenced Geldenhuys to five death sentences and three life sentences, plus 23 years.

During this time, I met James, a Police Sergeant stationed outside our house to protect us against the serial killer. His gentle personality immediately attracted me. The meekness he portrayed made me think of Jesus. Jesus illustrated meekness, but not weakness. I was very fragile and needed someone who could handle me gently. I opened my vulnerable heart to him and so our relationship began.

Then something truly dramatic happened in my personal life. I did not see this coming. My mother visited me to share a secret she kept to herself for many years. She told me she made a mistake many years ago, and that God wanted her to reveal the truth. The hurt and remorse were visible on her face and I became anxious about what she was going to tell me now. I then suspected that I was going to hear that I was adopted because I had always wondered why my two brothers and I were so different.

With obvious feelings of guilt in her eyes, she told me that Fanie was not my biological father. At the Church office, she developed a relationship with the local pastor, which later led to intimacy. I am the pastor's child! It felt as though I was in a Twilight Zone. An indefinite division between reality and fantasy became like the Twilight Zone between night and day. There is light outside, and yet, the sun is below the horizon. The German word *unheimlich* best describes how I felt. *Unheimlich* refers to something that is both known and unknown at the same time. I somehow knew I was different and then realised why I always felt different.

Hearing this truth was challenging. I had a battle to not judge my mother. Jesus tells us to look at our sins before judging someone else. The Bible teaches us we are to confront others' sins with truth, love and respect. God knows our human nature and warned us 37 times in the Bible to not judge others. A very firm warning appears in Mark 7: "Do not judge, or you too will be judged…" Years later, I eventually made contact with the pastor.

and will tell you more about that when we reach that point in my story.

In the meantime, my relationship with James developed. My spiritual conviction kept me from living with a man outside of marriage. I was also adamant about getting Dean back with me. James and I got married in October of that year. His gentle personality did not last long and changed to abnormal aggression that left me dumbstruck. My Calvinist approach to marriage and my deepest desire to get Dean back with me forced me to endure James's aggression.

Through all this drama, God blessed me with my second son, Michael, in August 1994. It was God's gift to my shattered heart and I will remain forever grateful that He came to bless my broken heart with the birth of Michael. A further blessing was that Jannie, my boss who later became my partner at the recruitment agency, agreed that I could work from home to take care of Michael. I did the permanent placements, and he did the contract placements. I will always be grateful to Jannie for his kindness.

I asked God to intercede on my behalf to get Dean back. It happened when I studied the book of James in the Bible. It taught me to not ask God for help and then continue with my efforts. This was probably one of the most important lessons in my life and I have to share this life-giving law in the Bible with you. It can change your life!

Bad things happen to us and test whether we truly trust the Lord. When you are not sure what is the right thing to do, ask God and then leave it to Him to deal with. Expect and know that He will help you. People who doubt whether God will really listen to them are like waves in the sea. The wind blows that wave back and forth. Do not doubt the Lord, for if you do so, you will not receive what you ask!

A mere ten days after I left the struggle about Dean in the hands of the Lord, the woman in George's life called me when Dean was with me for the weekend. She said I should not let George intimidate me and should keep Dean permanently because George had no real legal standing to keep him and often left him in her care. Finally, my boys shared the same home! Thank you, Lord!

James's aggression continued, and one day he even held a pistol to my head. His eyes seemed dense and unfathomable. It was impossible to determine what he was thinking or what he intended to do. A feeling of disbelief, mixed with fear and frustration, consumed me. I couldn't believe what was happening and part of me wondered whether I was dreaming or transported into the middle of some action movie. Fear crept in as my imagination started painting scenarios of what might happen to me. It is highly frustrating to feel you have no control over a situation. The welfare of my boys consumed my mind, and I put my life in the hands of the Lord, for I knew nothing would happen to me if it was not within His will.

As unbelievable as it may sound, my marriage with James continued. He resigned from the Police and we moved to Edenvale. We rented a house that I could also use as an office. In 1994, I started my recruitment company, JOY Placements and worked for myself until 1998. Grace Personnel approached me to come and work for them in my area. I had to manage the Ster-Kinekor contract for them.

James moved from job to job and always blamed his employers, never himself. He was simply too lazy to work and expected me to carry the financial burden of our household. James revealed narcissistic behaviour. Truth was a foreign concept to him and he was never sorry because he perceived himself as perfect. He viewed himself as superior to everyone and developed a pathological sense of self-entitlement. He became very aggressive if I dared to question him.

The situation became intolerable. Prayers did not have any effect, and it led me to believe that God expected me to endure my loveless marriage. One day I was listening to Corrie Ten Boom on the Radio Pulpit channel. I will never forget her words: "Worry does not empty tomorrow of its sorrow; it empties today of its strength." She continued to explain that if you pray about something that doesn't want to work, maybe God doesn't want it in your life.

Her words stuck in me and I started asking the Lord if he wanted me to leave this loveless marriage or carry on. One morning I woke up and felt the presence of the Holy Spirit. It truly felt as though God was dwelling within me. It was what our Hebrew brethren refer to as a Shekhinah moment. The Bible mentions several places where people experienced a Shekhinah moment, including the story of Moses and the burning bush. I could immediately sense that He did not want me to be abused, but also that I should leave it for Him to deal with in His way and time.

A few weeks later, James' brother offered him a job in Vereeniging, which he accepted. To our relief, he only came home over weekends. In June 2002, he asked me if it would be better for us if he did not come home over weekends anymore. I agreed immediately!

Grace Personnel then asked me to move to Cape Town to assist them. My boss, Craig, was not agreeable at first, but when I told him I was going through a divorce, he changed his mind. He decided it would be better for us to start afresh in Cape Town. Dean was a prefect at school, which made it difficult, but he immediately agreed that we should move to Cape Town.

We got divorced on 30 November that year and moved to Hout Bay, a suburb in Cape Town. Craig even paid for our move to Cape Town. Dean and Michael joined the Kronendal Primary School. It is a lovely co-educational, government school with a rich heritage dating back to 1901. And, behold, Dean became a prefect again in Kronendal Primary School!

After all that happened, I wish to share an important life lesson that I have learned through all these events. God's timing is always perfect. Our perception of time does not influence God. There are two different New Testament Greek words for time: Chronos and Kairos. The word Chronos refers to the general process of time or chronological time. As humans, we think of time in terms of days and hours. The word Kairos refers to the right time, or God's perfect timing. When God intervenes in our life, Chronos becomes Kairos' timing. He simply tests our perseverance and faithfulness before He shifts us into a new season. He therefore transforms Chronos time into Kairos time, His perfect time.

I went through a challenging Chronos season with James and with George. It was frustrating, but I did not lose my faith. If we keep our faith and do what is necessary in these challenging Chronos times in our lives, God will shift it into a Kairos season of reaping. Galatians 6: 9 teaches us, "Let us not lose heart in doing good, for in due time (Kairos) we shall reap if we do not grow weary."

My new season started in Cape Town. Please join me in this season of my life and learn how life can take us on routes we could not even imagine...

FIVE

We settled in the historical suburb of Hout Bay and loved to live there. We acquainted ourselves with the village by exploring our neighbourhood and learning its history. The name Hout Bay dates back to 1653. Hout Bay, or Houtbaai, so named by the Dutch settler's literary means "Wood Bay". It was a beautiful tree-rich valley filled with many matured yellowwood trees. The trees became the primary source of timber for historical buildings, such as the Castle of Good Hope. Protective mountains and an excellent fishing area made it ever so popular. They probably established the fishing village of Hout Bay in about 1867 when a German immigrant, Jacob Trautman, began to farm and fish in the area.

The combination of the sea, mountains, nature and a friendly community created a perfect home for us. The rising and setting of the sun is a spectacular show in Hout Bay. In summer, the sun sets slowly. It ignites the sky with fiery colours of red, orange, pink and purple. Looking at the sunset calms your nerves. The beautiful sunrise is striking and bold. It symbolises hope and renewal and energises you for the day.

The boys did well in school and were happy. When your children are happy, life is simply easier. I worked for Grace Personnel Agency until 2002 when I became so sick, that I could not work anymore. The doctors could not find the source of my sickness and later diagnosed it as a stress-related sickness. I believe God wanted me to rest and spend more quality time in His presence. Rest is important to our spiritual walk with the Lord, and we need to appreciate the value of rest. Rest allows our mind, body, and spirit to renew. It strengthens us and helps us to focus. An important part of our rest is to trust the Lord. As the prophet Isaiah rightly said, "Those who hope in the LORD will renew their strength. They will soar on wings like eagles; they will run and not grow weary; they will walk and not be faint."

Reading this Scripture of Isaiah made me think of eagles through spiritual eyes. Eagles know no limits or boundaries. It is said that eagles are the only bird that embraces the turbulence to push itself higher. When other birds flee from the weather, the eagle actively engages stronger winds to fly high above storms instead of seeking shelter.

I thought about the many versions of the story of the eagle that grew up with partridges, or chickens in another version. Anyway, the eagle baby ended up with chickens or partridges. They raised him because they thought he was one of them. One day, whilst playing with his feathered mates he saw an eagle flying in the sky. He asked who the bird soaring through the sky was and expressed his desire to fly as well. His feathered mates said that he was one of them and could never fly like that in the sky. The moral of the story is that he was born as an eagle but conditioned to think like a partridge or chicken.

This is a sad story. We become what we believe we are. It reminded me of the Wisdom of Solomon that warns us: "Keep your heart with all vigilance, for from it flow the springs of life." We have to be careful what we think because our thoughts determine our lives. Our thoughts become our words, for we speak what we think. Our words then become our actions and form our habits that ultimately determine our destiny.

I find it fascinating to see how the impact of one story spiritually leads me to another story to confirm how the Lord wants to renew my mind and strength. To confirm that I must be careful how I think led to another story that an Indian chief taught his grandson about the two wolves inside us.

"A fight is going on inside me. It is a terrible fight, and it is between two wolves. One is evil - he is anger, sorrow, hate, greed, arrogance and cruelty. The other is good - he is joy, hope, love, generosity, humility and kindness. This same fight is going on inside you and inside every other person, too."

The grandson asked his grandfather, "Which wolf will win?" The old chief replied, "The one you feed."

Thinking about the time I became sick, and all I learned in that season brings a smile to my face today, for it renewed my thinking and led to a burst of energy. In 2003, I started Ithemba to create a programme to train prospective entrepreneurs. iThemba means 'hope' in isiZulu. Ithemba also means 'hope', 'trust', and 'faith' in Xhosa. This is Biblical.

I sought sponsors, but political figures who wanted to control the flow of money blocked me. In 2003, when I started Ithemba, the government introduced the Broad-Based Black Economic Empowerment (B-BBEE) Act, No. 53 of 2003. The fundamental objective of this Act is to advance the economic participation of black people in the South African economy.

I was a white girl in the so-called new South Africa and did not fit the preference that the politics of the day granted to non-white people. My motives were pure because I truly wanted to empower historically disadvantaged people. I wanted to teach them how to become the masters of their destiny.

I understand the need for economic transformation. However, I also believe that white people with good business acumen have a responsibility to transform the economic landscape in South Africa. Empowering previously disadvantaged people will eventually lead to an equal distribution of wealth. Our country will never be a good place for any of us unless it is a good place for all of us.

Sadly, history has shown us many examples of mismanagement and corruption. The money never reaches the intended recipients. I am not politically inclined and do not wish to continue this discussion. My only concern is that we should not forget why a revolution against Apartheid came about. It has everything to do with fairness. Unfairness is the reason behind most revolutions in the world's history.

In the same manner, a lesson will repeat itself until it is learned and applied, something that is not fair will also not disappear. C. J. Langenhoven, an Afrikaans poet, described it as follows (loosely translated): Nothing is ever finally settled that is not fairly settled. If you grew up on a farm and have ever milked in a bucket, you will know that you can shake the bucket all you want, but the cream will always rise to the top.

If the flow of money in South Africa does not truly empower the masses, then another revolution will start.

Also, if young white people, who were not part of apartheid, are excluded from opportunities just because they are white, then we repeat Apartheid and its unfair and negative consequences.

I repeat, our country will never be a good place for any of us unless it is a good place for all of us. What we need are leaders who truly care about the future of our country. We need true stewards. Stewards that do the right things today to create a better tomorrow for all our people. Stewards never enrich themselves to the detriment of others. I love Warren Buffett's opinion of true Stewardship. He said: "Someone's sitting in the shade today because someone planted a tree a long time ago."

Irrespective of political interference with Ithemba, the Cape Argus Business Day published an article about it. As they say, when one door closes, another one opens. RSG and SAFM also invited me for radio interviews.

Later on, I did an interview at Tygerberg Christian radio station, which delivered an unintended but exciting result. Someone from the Cape Town Traffic Department listened to my interview and asked me to address their conference as a guest speaker. I supported them in various ways afterwards. It is amazing to see how a window opens to some opportunity I could never have thought about beforehand. As they say, The Lord moves in mysterious ways. I have learned to not try to kick doors open. The Lord will keep doors closed if He so wishes, irrespective of how hard I kick! He then loves to surprise you with doors that open that you cannot claim you had opened yourself. I am sure the Lord has a sense of humour with His children!

Swisscontact then contacted me out of the blue. I did not even know about their existence. It is a Swiss non-profit- foundation, established in 1959 by exponents of the Swiss private sector. They unleash the potential of private initiative to foster sustainable development and shared prosperity in developing and emerging economies. Their development work focuses on private sector-led, sustainable economic development. The aim is to improve the quality of life for all in developing and emerging countries. A key focus is to strengthen the skills of individuals and foster the competitiveness of companies.

Swisscontact offers customised consultancy and capacity development services. They also provide funds for economically sustainable service providers. They seek appropriate individuals whom they can train to deliver services in their community before they release any funds. Swisscontact approached me as a service provider to SMMEs. I had to undergo their programme and prepare a business plan before they would release funds.

Then Nedbank, one of our country's major commercial banks, nominated me as businesswoman of the Western Cape. The woman who nominated me at Nedbank requested me to assist her with her green projects in the Helderberg area. I accepted her offer to gain more stability and a steady income while I continued with the Swisscontact programme. To overcome the long distance between Hout Bay and the Helderberg, we moved from Hout Bay to Gordons Bay.

In May 2004, I sold my big car and replaced it with a smaller, more affordable car. I did not arrange insurance before I fetched the car. A mistake I will never make again because ended up in an absolutely frightening accident. I lost control of my car on the mountain pass between Rooi-Els and Gordon's Bay.

Some of you might not know this mountain pass, so let me explain it. This mountain pass offers a splendid scenic coastal drive between the windswept village of Rooi-Els and the naval town of Gordons Bay. This lovely coastal drive stretches between the two towns over 21 km. The pass contains 77 bends, curves and corners of which four are over 150 degrees.

Let me make something very clear. This mountain pass is high above the sea. Any motorist with a rational mind will slow down because the last thing you want to happen is to lose control on this road to plunge into the sea far below.

And then it happened to me! Something went wrong with my car that caused me to lose control. My car went over the side of the mountain pass and tumbled down towards the sea. The car bounced over the rocks on the cliff and came to a stop a few meters from the sea. The car was a total wreck, but I was unharmed. There is no other way to describe it than simply generous grace from the Lord. In the most distressing moment in my life, God was there because only He could save me in such a miraculous way.

For a period after the accident, the Lord exposed me to the goodness of people. I couldn't afford a car again and the people of Gordons Bay immediately stepped in to take care of my children and get them to the places they needed to be. I developed a new appreciation for my fellow human beings and experienced how they served me and my children, as Jesus teaches us to do. The words of Jesus, that He came to serve and not to be served, found physical form in my life through the good deeds of the surrounding people. I am truly thankful.

My life after the accident continued with peaks and valleys, as we all experience in life and the business world. My priority was to complete the Swisscontact project. I invite you to experience the impact of this project and other events in the next season of my life ...

SIX

Hout Bay stole my heart. Our move from Hout Bay to Gordons Bay was for practical reasons. Gordons Bay's community support to our family during difficult times made the move from Hout Bay to Gordons Bay easier. Gordon's Bay also has a rich history and many unique attractions.

Gordonsbaai was previously called Vissersbaai (Fisher's Bay) by the Dutch due to the abundance of fish caught under Cape Hangklip. Gordon's Bay derived its name from Colonel Robert Jacob Gordon. He was the commander of the VOC Garrison during the first British occupation of the Cape in 1795. British colonialism has left its footprints here, and elsewhere in South Africa.

The farmland around the bay's ownership varied between several families. Ownership began with Catherine Cloete, the widow of Jan van Brienen. Many years later, the Miller family became an institution in the developing town and was involved with the Town Management Board since it was established in 1902, as well as the Municipality established in 1961.

The Hottentots Hollands Mountain range watches over the town, with the Steenbras Dam at the top of the mountain. Gordon's Bay is north-facing, which means sun all day long. The beams of the rising sun cast a rosy colour over the ocean. It creates a beautiful contrast between the blueness of the water and the whiteness of the sand. Gordons Bay is one of the top destinations to watch the sunset in Cape Town. Bikini Beach, a romantic setting, is an exceptional place to watch the sunset at Gordon's Bay.

I continued with the Swisscontact project. Without a car, it was challenging. My new learning curve was huge. I could not afford to hire a taxi and had to learn to ride with the much cheaper common taxis. They transport people between townships and different destinations in the city. They pick you up at certain places, almost like a bus stop. I had to learn which taxi to take to get me to the right destination. It was nerve-wracking but also an exciting experience. My fellow passengers were friendly and quickly taught me how to take advantage of these taxis.

In June, Swisscontact informed me that I was one of the five finalists and had to present to the people of Switzerland in Cape Town. Money was scarce, and I had to take the train to do the presentation. The Strand's train station was the closest to me and I had to walk the 10 km from Gordons Bay to the train station. I put on my best clothes and started walking to the station. My neighbour noticed me walking and stopped his car. He enquired as to where I was going in such fancy clothes. After I indicated my destination, he smiled and told me to get in so that he could drive me through to the station. My lifelong friend Magda from Gauteng then paid R1000 into my account. I still think about these human angels who helped me through the difficult times.

A month later, Swisscontact announced me as the winner. Amen! In October they gave me a car and also R70 000 to buy equipment to continue with Ithemba. I rented a small building in Gordons Bay and started supporting upcoming businesses. I involved partners so that we could specialise in the different facets of business, for example, marketing, financial management, and so on. Working with partners was a challenge on its own and I quickly learned to do things myself instead.

I went to Johannesburg where I met Chris of BNI, Business Network International. He referred me to André Diederichs, who was at the helm of Old Mutual's focus on the business market. I had a plan to create a one-stop service for small businesses and explored the idea with him. Large companies opposed the App that I wanted to create. André taught me important business lessons and in 2011 also started his consulting firm André's love for the Lord and his sound business principles established a lasting friendship between us.

Over the next five years, I tried various things, but nothing produced substantial results. History is full of entrepreneurs who failed and became discouraged. We can learn, though, from those who refused to give up on their passion despite repeatedly enduring failure and rejection.

Sketch a picture in your head where you are sitting in front of a group of bankers. You tell them you're going to build a multibillion-dollar business based on a mouse, a fairy, and seven dwarfs, and then ask them to help you achieve that goal. This situation was not just a picture inside a certain young man's head. It happened, and the bankers laughed at him. His brother, Roy, also always tried to put brakes on his dream and passion by accusing him of madness.

This did not stop the young entrepreneur from passionately pursuing his dream. He had hired engineers, with his own money and they secretly met after working hours to fulfil this dream. This young man, as you could probably already deduce, was Walt Disney, which is an example of passion and unprecedented dedication.

Another profound example is that of Thomas Edison. He pioneered the method of technological research and invented electric lighting and the phonograph. It was his attitude that made him a winner. Thomas Edison taught his assistants an important lesson about how one should respond to failures. His assistants said: "We have just completed our seven hundredth experiment and we still do not have a solution. We failed."

"No, my friends," said Edison, "you have not failed. You just know more about the subject than anyone else on earth. And we are now closer to the answer because we now know that we no longer need to do those 700 experiments." He added: "Don't call it failure. Call it training." I do not know how much extra effort it required before Edison achieved success. In South Africa, Eskom does not have to learn to generate electricity. They must just learn to keep the electricity on!

Business, like life, is a training school. Look at the turtle: He only makes progress when he sticks his head out. The same goes for entrepreneurs. They will only make progress if they are willing to never stop learning and to take action.

The business world is dynamic and keeps on changing. Lifelong learning is not a choice anymore. Everyone makes mistakes, every day. If we learn from our mistakes, then mistakes become our best teachers. Only those who do nothing do not make mistakes. Mistakes are an inextricable part of life and business. Remember the words of Charter Kettering: "You will never stub your toe while standing. The faster you walk, the more likely you are to stub your toe and the more likely you are to get somewhere."

We should worry more about the things we didn't do rather than the things we did wrong. Never say: "I wanted to do something". Do what you have to do and rather say: "I did something!" A girl wrote a very poignant little poem during the Vietnam War. It illustrates the tragic consequences of an attitude towards life that is aimed at saying: "If only...". I want to share this important life lesson with you.

Things you didn't do
Remember the day I borrowed your car and dented it?
I thought you'd kill me, but you didn't.
And the time I'd drag you to the beach and
you said it would rain, and it did.
I thought you'd say I told you so, but you didn't.
And the time I flirted with all the guys to make
you jealous, and you were.
I thought you'd leave me, but you didn't.
And do you remember the time I spilled blueberry pie all over your new car?
I thought you'd smack me, but you didn't.
And the time I forgot to tell you the dance was formal and you showed up in jeans?
I thought you'd leave me forever, but you didn't.
Yes, there were lots of things you didn't do,
but you put up with me, and loved me, and protected me.
And there were so many things
I wanted to make up to you when you'd come home from Vietnam -
but you didn't!

This poem gripped my soul and made me realise once again that we must not neglect to do the things that are necessary to keep our dreams alive. True entrepreneurs will keep on trying new things and avoid the question of: "Things I didn't do." What eventually makes entrepreneurs successful is their tenacity and patience. God certainly taught me patience!

Inspiration from an unexpected source led me to the next season in my life. I can't help but smile when I think about it. I was in the gym working out with my earphones on. The next moment, the Rock song Butterflies and Hurricanes by Muse, started playing. The words in the song immediately appealed to me. Especially the words: "Don't let yourself down. Don't let yourself go. You've got to be the best. You've got to change the world and use this chance to be heard. Your time is now."

The words sunk in and made me wonder why the song's name is *Butterflies and Hurricanes* I really couldn't think what butterflies had in common with hurricanes. They are polar opposites. I told André about it. He smiled and said it made sense from a business's point of view. Hurricanes create storm surges. It can destroy everything in its path. Sometimes it feels as if hurricanes confront us. Butterflies fly leisurely around and are non-threatening. As you say, the opposite of hurricanes.

While listening to him, something else about butterflies suddenly became clear to me. I interrupted him eagerly: "Wait, there is something I forgot about butterflies. Their life is not just smooth sailing and non-threatening. They have their battles. To escape their cocoons, they must struggle to free their bodies. The struggle is so intense that the butterfly may seem near death, but it is this very struggle that creates the beautiful butterfly. Butterflies also face their own hurricanes!"

André chuckled, "Yes you are right! There is also an economic law that is referred to as *the butterfly effect*. It suggests that small actions can lead to yield substantial rewards in the future."

That discussion energised me and that is when I decided to make the move to start a new business venture. I invite you to the next season of my life when I woke up with an idea that was like a sleeping giant within me …

SEVEN

In 2012, I founded the Business Directive Development Group (Pty) Ltd. I would like to share some important life and business lessons with you before I expand on what has been happening with my new business venture. Events and lessons influence us on our life path. It affects the way we think and do things.

Life has taught me that failing doesn't mean you'll never succeed. Patience is truly a virtue. You just have to remain committed to your goal. If you go sailing and the wind dies down, you have a choice. You can wait and hope for wind, or you can start paddling. It takes longer, but you will reach the side.

One of humanity's greatest challenges is fear of failure. In the business world, this fear can also prevent you from taking chances. It takes courage to take chances. People's view of risk varies widely and is subjective. For example, a person might consider it risky to jump from a plane with a parachute but have much less fear of pursuing a new business idea.

Those of us who want to be an entrepreneur must surely have the courage to explore business ideas. There is a strong comparison between the risk of starting a new business and the unpredictable life cycle of a lobster. For a business to survive and thrive during its critical first three to five years, requires more than a good business idea. It takes real courage. Let us learn from the lobster!

Sea conditions, like market conditions, can determine

how long it takes for a lobster or a business to reach maturity. The West Coast lobster requires approximately six to nine years, while the East Coast lobster reaches maturity in just three years. However, the first few years of a lobster's life are very uncertain as only 10 out of 10 000 eggs survive. This equates to 0. 01%! Start-up businesses also have a high failure rate during their critical years, with a mere 25% surviving this period.

It's the years between birth and maturity that take real courage. The lobster sheds its shell up to 25 times in its first five years. Lobsters need their shell to ensure predators do not rip them apart. However, if they do not shed their shells, they cannot grow and the shell will become their prison and eventually their coffin. Can you imagine how vulnerable that lobster must feel when it sheds its shell? Start-up businesses experience similar periods of vulnerability in the first few years, with less vulnerability once the business platform is firmly established. I trust you will now look at the lobster on your plate with much more appreciation!

I experienced many vulnerable episodes during my lifetime and am certainly not fond of failure. To me, it is vital to learn from your mistakes to avoid the same mistakes. You will know you have learned the lesson when your actions adjust. One lesson of life is that if one does not want to hear, you will feel! It reminds me of the story of the man who fell into the hole. The story, in five chapters, goes like this:

Chapter 1: I'm on the road. There is a deep hole. I fall into it. I feel lost and desperate, it's not my fault. It takes me a long time to get out of the hole.

Chapter 2: I'm on the same path. There is a deep hole. I pretend not to see the hole. I fall into the hole again. I can't believe I'm in the same hole. It's not my fault. It takes me a long time to get out of the hole.

Chapter 3: I'm on the same path. There is a deep hole. I see the hole is there. I fall into the hole again. I cannot help it, it's a habit. But then I see where I am. I know it's my fault. I get out of the hole quickly.

Chapter 4: I am on the same path. There is a deep hole. I walk around the hole.

Chapter 5: I walk a different path!
When I founded Business Directive Development Group (Pty) Ltd in 2012, I still provided services for entrepreneurs. However, in 2013, I moved back to my roots in the business world, namely human resources and recruitment.

The expression *better the devil you know than the devil you don't,* can refer to people or things. The proverb, *let the cobbler stick to his last,* means that one should do the work one is an expert at. Apparently, Apelles, a famous painter in the year 400 BC, formulated this expression in reaction to a cobbler who criticised the sandals in his painting.

It started when I reacted to an advert for a recruitment consultant to manage their company. They had only one client. The agency operated from Tyger Valley, in the Northern suburbs of Cape Town about 55 km from Gordons Bay. I joined them as a service provider through Business Directive Development Group (Pty) Ltd, and not as an employee. I invoiced them. My salary was low, and I soon tapped into my entrepreneurial spirit by negotiating a deal where I receive a percentage of all the new business we gain. Incentives drive me to work harder.

When I started there, our monthly turnover was only R11 600. Then the sleeping giant within me woke up. Success has a way to breed more success. I experienced how total focus on a task can change small initial successes into a wave of successes that becomes larger and larger. When I left them in 2018, our turnover was over R8 million per month!

Over that same period, I rid myself of all my debt and could continue with a clean slate. I replaced my old car with a more fuel-sufficient car and bought my first property in Somerset-West.

For the first time, I could go overseas. Venice, known also as the "City of Canals," was my first overseas experience. The city's winding canals, striking architecture, and beautiful bridges left me breathless. The English poet Samuel Rogers describes the dreamlike fairytale qualities that Venice espouses in this poem. "There is a glorious City in the Sea.

> The Sea is in the broad, the narrow streets,
> Ebbing and flowing; and the salt sea-weed
> Clings to the marble of her palaces.
> No track of men, no footsteps to and fro,
> Lead to her gates. The path lies o'er the Sea,
> Invisible; and from the land we went,
> As to a floating City – steering in,
> And gliding up her streets as in a dream…"

The uncountable pigeons in Saint Marcus Square are also an overwhelming experience. They say that pigeons once rivalled cats as the mascots of Venice. I could see it and I could feel why! The way they come and sit all over your body is a bewildering experience. Pigeons are, if not sacred, at least highly respected in Venice and they can get away with almost anything.

I also visited Croatia and travelled by ship for ten days around the Greek islands. One of my most precious memories is when I flew to Prague to meet with my youngest son, Michael. We went to Budapest in Hungary where his birth father's family is from. We also met in Georgia later that year. To spend time with your child while experiencing overseas countries is a double abundance for me.

A highlight for me was visiting Israel in 2018 with the Covenant Fellowship Church International Bible College Tour. I studied theology and completed my fifth and sixth-year studies through them. My love for the Word of God and businesses came together when I completed my Honours Mini Dissertation during the pandemic. Jewish folk have a long history of highly successful business practices. My Dissertation sought an answer to the following question. "Could Judaic principles lead to greater success if applied to Christian-owned business practices?"

Research proved that the Jewish nation is proportionally far more successful than most other nations. Strong ethics, love for God and man, and servant leadership formed the foundation for the proposed solution in the study. Proverbs teach us that wisdom is the principal thing. Being prosperous is part of a loving covenant with God and not a result of cunning business practices. Today's society teaches differently. I have found the reverence towards God of the Judaic system tremendously attractive and an answer to the deep desire to worship Him with a pure, yet bold spirit.

Israel was an amazing experience. I remember thinking about Jesus, or Yeshua on my way to Israel. I've learned that Christian means "like Christ," or "anointed one," as the Greeks refer to Him. In Hebrew, it is Mashiach or Messiah, as we pronounce it. I wondered how Yeshua looked in His human form. I have seen so many versions of Him in movies. Jesus walked a lot and worked in the building trade when there were no power tools. He must have been strong and muscular. He would have dressed as a typical Hebrew man in those days and did not look different in any crowd. Therefore, Judas had to kiss Him to identify Him.

I was looking forward to learning more about the culture of Jewish people and discovering the underlying treasures in the Bible. Much to my surprise, Israel is no longer a desolate desert land. It changed into a prosperous and fruitful country, as the ancient prophets foretold us. What sticks with me is the size of this tiny country that causes so much uproar in the world. If you stand on Mount Olive, you can see the Dead Sea from there.

One highlight was when we entered the Old City of Jerusalem. I remember whispering, "This is not the telling or the reading history. This is history." The Western Wall in the old city is worth visiting. The Western Wall is also known as the Kotel or the Wailing Wall. It is the only remaining part of the wall of the Temple built by King Solomon.

It overwhelmed me to see the Jews standing in front of the wall. They weep and pray while moving their bodies back and forth. One could imagine how they call on the God of their ancestors. They prayed for the peace of Jerusalem and for the Mashiach to come.

There were many other highlights, but my baptism in the Jordan River was an unforgettable spiritual experience. The water was surprisingly cool and there were a lot of fish that nibbled my feet. Relax, they're not dangerous and it is healthy. Small fishes come and eat your dead skin, which rejuvenates your skin. I must mention that it tickles when they nibble on your feet. Those of you who are sensitive to ticklish things might find this experience a bit awkward. Being baptised in the river where John baptised Jesus will remain a highlight in my life.

I am truly thankful that I could learn the positive impact of focusing on a goal with tenacity. Tenacity accompanied by trust in the Lord and myself during my time with the recruitment company from 2013 to 2018. This lesson reminds me of the remarkable cooperation between the hummingbird and the flower. It is undoubtedly one of the most appropriate examples of how total dedication rewards you.

The hummingbird does not fly around from flower to flower, but hovers like a helicopter over a particular flower. It allows the bird to pollinate it while its wings ceaselessly flutter.

With enough time at the flower, the hummingbird gets sufficient access to the pollen. And, in return, the flower compensates the hummingbird with an increased delivery of nectar. It also creates a multiplying effect because the proper pollination process creates more flowers for the future. Total focus and dedication breed success, which breeds more success. This is like the hummingbird's dedication that multiplies the flowers.

In most of our lives, work, family, and friendship consume our time. The world of businesses, my faith, and my children are at the centre of my life. Motherhood is an important part of my life. The extraordinary men that my two sons became are probably my most important legacy. Please join me on this precious journey…

EIGHT

Giving life is a Divine miracle. It changed my perception of love and care forever. Every person is a miracle because each person is unique. While there might be some similarities between people, no two people are alike. Each person has a unique personality, perspective, and set of experiences that make them different from everyone else. I love the way the poet in Psalm describes the uniqueness of every person. *For You have possessed my inward parts; You wove me in the womb of my mother. I will thank You, for with awesome ways I am distinguished; Your works are marvellous, and my soul knows it very well.* The Creator even knows our hearts and our thoughts!

God creates every person with a divine purpose, and we all have a unique message to bring and a special act of love to perform. Sometimes we travel far and wide to see natural wonders such as wildlife, mountains, rivers, and oceans. But we walk past the mirror without turning to look twice. We easily ignore the wonder of our uniqueness.

Each of our children has a wonderfully unique anatomy. They have a unique God-given personality and they are a once-off gift to humanity that will never return or be repeated. They have a song to sing and a gift to offer that is unique to them!

The greatest gift we as parents can give our children is to allow them to express their uniqueness and originality. Allow them to be who they are because no one can be exactly like them! We should also try to instil good values in them so that wrong influences do not engulf them.

Parenting does not come with a manual, and a parent's responsibility is frighteningly large. It forced me as a mother daily on my knees. In the early stages with my two sons, I realised that no two people are the same. Every person is a unique gift from God, and the way we embrace that gift is what brings the best out of them. I was a single mother since they were very young. It is not easy being a single parent. I had to make many decisions on my own. It was challenging to make decisions that a father should naturally make. As single mothers, we need wisdom to deal with the many questions in life. I have learned that embracing their unique gifts, encouraging them, and loving them unconditionally has helped them to make good decisions in life.

André's Afrikaans book, *Nalatenskap* (Legacy), left a big impression on me as a mother. It's a story of wrong decisions that led to broken relationships between parents and children. Decisions that come back to haunt you later. There are two leading stories in this book. The first story is about Willem van der Merwe, who is a farmer in Ficksburg. He had a huge falling out with his only son Wilhelmus about his choice of a wife and as a result, had no contact with his son for over twenty years. Wilhelmus and his Scottish wife, Allison, moved to Scotland where he farmed with his father-in-law, Craig Mackenzie. In the meantime, two grandchildren were also born that Willem and his wife Lenie were not aware of. Willem became very ill with cancer and he desperately wanted to find his son in Scotland to reconcile the family. The story takes the reader through all the intrigues to reconcile the family.

The letter to his son pleading for his forgiveness sent me on an emotional rollercoaster. I want to share this story with you and loosely translate it into English.

My Dear Son.
I sit in front of a blank piece of paper in the morning hours and try to put my deep hurt and feelings of guilt into words. Over the years, I believed that one day you and I would bury the hatchet. Well, Father Wisdom also came to teach me that it won't happen if I don't try to make it happen. ONE DAY has been confronting me for quite some time now because ONE DAY HAS ALREADY COME, and I am bitterly sorry that it took me so long to realise it.

Guilt is like a cancer that gets worse over time. It eats at me because I struggle to find the words to soften the deep hurt that I've caused to both of us. Yesterday I read Ingrid Jonker's Afrikaans poem, "Bitterbessie Dagbreek" (Bitter Berry Daybreak). The words touched me intensely and deeply. It's as if I taste the bitter berry daily and it's as if it gets more bitter as I get angry with myself for my thoughtless words that caused the separation between us.

The words in the poem remind me of my infinite longing and deepest heart's desire that my destructive words of the past should just please stop echoing in my mind. I yearn to replace my unforgivable words, which hurt so intensely, with how I feel about you. You are my firstborn, my only son, and I love you more than life itself. Being your father is the greatest blessing in my life, and I trampled it with my ridiculously inflated ego. An ego destroyed my longing to be able to hold you just one more time and beg for forgiveness.

Faan, our foreman who you will remember from your childhood, asked me yesterday for the umpteenth time when you were coming home one day. It broke me and I shared my heart with him. The pain was visible on his face and upset me a lot.

Later that day, I saw him on his knees, praying out loud. The simplicity of his prayer took me completely by surprise. He prayed, "Afternoon Lord, it's old Faan here. I am looking for a little attention please and hope you are not angry with me because I have a favour to ask today. Boss Willem's heart is broken with his boy's departure. I don't know the place where he is, but I think you will be able to find him and talk to his heart. Please tell him his father's heart is hurting, and he has to come home now because the farm doesn't feel right without him. Tell him old Faan asks that."

My son, I don't know where you are and am writing this letter to you this morning because I don't know if I will ever have the opportunity to tell you this in person. A wise person said that the saddest words are often not spoken. Staying silent about something that needs to be addressed brings heartache and I can no longer stay silent knowing that it perpetuates the hurt. I hope that one day you will be able to read this and forgive my foolishness from so many years ago.

My son, I was wrong to force you to choose between Allison and us. I pray that you will be able to forgive me and that you are safe in the hands of our Lord. Son, I bear the pain I have caused to all; I pray that you will unite with our family, even if it is without me. Please forgive me. I love you son.
DAD

The story made me realise how careful we must be as parents not to dictate to our children who they choose as their life partners. If they are in love, then it dominates their thinking and emotions, and our interference can lead to eternal separation. It is naturally difficult for a parent!

The second story reminds me of my story about my biological father that I did not know about until my mother told me. My mother visited me to share this secret she kept to herself for many years. She told me that Fanie was not my biological father.

This second story is about Dries Beukes, a farmer in Middelburg, Mpumalanga. He is a conservative person who serves on the church council. Dries and Lisa are happily married and have a close bond with their two sons, Driesman and Dawid. Years ago, Dries attended the Oktoberfest in Germany with a student tour. During the tour, under Bacchus's influence, he stepped over the line with a German girl, Marichen. As a Christian, the incident deeply troubled his conscience. He simply flew back to South Africa the next day and proceeded to ban the thoughtless act from his mind. Twenty-five years later, his daughter Brigitte, whom he did not know about, walks into his office in Middelburg. A lot of drama then follows.

I can truly imagine how Brigitte must have felt when her mother told her about her biological father in South Africa. In case you wonder. I met my biological father, and we spent some time together. However, he did not want his family and the community to know about me and severed all ties. The role my father Fanie played in my life and the love of my Heavenly Father eased the pain of knowing that my biological father did not want to recognise me as his daughter.

Let me now share my experience with you as a mother. Dean, my first child, was born in April 1989. The gift of life is second to none. Holding him in my arms and looking down at his face overwhelmed me with indescribable joy and love. God blessed Dean with multiple talents, a jack of all trades. He has many interests and creative pursuits. He did well in all kinds of sports, from cricket to hockey to rugby.

At a stage, he was not happy at the Hottentots-Holland High School, situated between the towns of Somerset-West and Strand. He wanted to change schools, but I taught him a life lesson that became a motto in our family. I taught him to never walk away from a defeat and only move on when he is victorious in what he does. Dean was young, but listened and reaped the rewards. He was captain of his school's younger hockey team and played for the first team on the same day. His coach took the team for hamburgers after the game to celebrate their victory. In the restaurant, the coach praised Dean for his good game. Dean was now ready to move on to a new school as a winner!

His sense of humour is infectious and endeared him to the children and teachers. One anecdote I remember was when his teacher called me because he hadn't submitted an assignment yet. He also had to go for a small eye operation and then turned up at school the next day with an eyepatch on his eye. He pointed to the eyepatch and told the teacher: "You shouldn't have called my mother. Look what happened to me!"

Dean was also very strong academically and wanted to finish school to enter the world of business. He aimed to join Somerset College. It is an independent English-speaking, co-educational high school in the Winelands of the Western Cape. The school follows the Cambridge syllabus and was very expensive to attend. I could not afford to pay the school fees at this stage in my life.

Dean then decided that it was time for his father to fulfil his fatherly duties and approached him to pay his school fees. His father agreed and paid the deposit. Dean joined the new school and finished his grade 11 and grade 12 in one year with excellent results. He even received a monetary reward for maths. Apart from his sports and academic talents, he also has musical talents and plays the guitar, bass guitar, and drums. School bands were a very popular trend in those days and kept him busy for a while before he moved on to pursue his dream of being a businessperson.

Travelling is in our blood, and Dean grabbed every opportunity to see the world. He even lived with Antionette in New Zealand before they started a health business in South Africa. His compassion for people became clear when he learned about the terrible living conditions of some of his staff. Dean and Antionette bought a flat in Somerset-West to create a better living for these staff and their family. He simply could not knowingly allow his colleagues to live in such terrible conditions.

They later moved to the USA and then ended up in Vancouver, Canada where he was appointed the CEO of a company called Tomorrow Foods. Dean is a brilliant businessperson that gets things done in the typical Nike manner of, "just do it!"

God blessed Dean and Antionette with Eden, their firstborn and my first grandchild! A grandchild is a precious gift and quickly overwhelms you. It's hard to describe the secret of a strong bond between a grandparent and a grandchild. You have to experience it to understand it. I am so grateful that I could visit Eden in Vancouver in 2022 and miss him every day. I wish the distance between us wasn't so big because I just want to hold him and let him understand how loved he is.

My second son, Michael, was born in August 1994. I was on a strong spiritual path and learned about the importance of names. The name Michael was constantly on my mind. Then people came from three different places and told me to call him Michael. Even Dean told me to call him Michael. I prayed about it and it felt like he was moving in my womb when I said the name. It probably sounds strange for people to hear this, but for me, it was a confirmation that I had to call him Michael.

From childhood, Michael has been very protective of me. I remember once we went on holiday and while walking on the beach, a crab came running towards us. Michael grabbed my hand and said: "Don't worry Mom, I will always be there to protect you. He is with me and will always watch over me. It reminds me of the Archangel Michael who defends us in a spiritual battle.

It's as if Michael's spirit connects to mine. Recently I went through a terrible time when someone tried to drag my name through the mud unjustifiably. Michael then had dreams about me being attacked and contacted me to find out what was going on. It's as if he could sense my inner turmoil.

Michael is a wise person. Money does not motivate him, but he takes good care of himself. He also studies social sciences as I did. He loves to study, read, and write stories. Both my sons act wisely but differ, in that Michael is a typical dreamer while Dean is a typical doer.

Michael loves travelling like the rest of us. He sold computers to fund his first overseas trip. He flew to Munich in Germany on Christmas Eve and was upgraded to first class on his very first overseas flight. How lucky can one be?! He travelled all over and fell in love with Europe and decided to settle in Brussels, Belgium. He is involved with Carolina, an intelligent and wise woman that I liked immediately. She holds an important government position in Brussels and even wrote one of their Laws.

Michael loves to meditate and have intelligent conversations. Although Michael is stationed in Brussels, he has always had a vested interest in my company. He plays a vital role in the technology division of our company and is important to the well-being of our company.

I had a special experience with Michael in 2022. After I visited Dean and his family in Vancouver, I explored Turkey with some of my dear friends and precious mentors during my theological studies, Doctors Simone and Johny Slabbert.

After the tour, Michael joined me in Antalya, Turkey. I rented a car, and I had to drive on the "wrong side" of the road. This was an exhilarating experience! We travelled along the coast to Kas and spent a precious week together. We just rested, as only Michael can lead me to rest.

I would like to end this chapter with the importance of our legacy. A legacy is not a mere inheritance. A legacy is not only what we leave BEHIND for our children. No, a legacy is also what we leave INSIDE our children. It is the values that we instil in them that will guide them in life. Values, such as integrity and ethical work habits will allow them to take care of themselves. If you teach them the importance of respect for others, it will foster sound relationships, since respect is the glue that keeps people together.

In the next chapter, I will elaborate on the events in my life that changed my business from small beginnings to a more substantial business. Please join me on this journey from good to greatness...

NINE

"Luck and destiny are the excuses for the world's failures," these are the famous words of Henry Ford. In 1896, the founder of Ford Motor Company built his first car and took it for a spin on the streets of Detroit.

Is luck and destiny an excuse for failure? Life may be easier for some people and unnecessarily difficult for others. During tough times, people may question the purpose of their hardships and feel envious of successful individuals. They might start thinking that luck and destiny are against them. They might also believe that successful people know some magical secret that they're hiding from them.

What I just described is the power that belief has over your life. I have mentioned the wisdom of Solomon before and want to repeat it. *"Above all else, guard your heart, for it is the wellspring of life" (Proverbs 4:23).* What we think or believe impacts our lives. Negative thoughts lead to negative words that you speak over yourself and then you start acting on your own words. Soon it will become a negative habit and, unless you change it, your life is going to end up fulfilling your own prophecy of failure.

Life has many facets, and you might fail in some facets but succeed in other facets. A businessperson might manage a highly successful business but fail as a parent or vice versa. Let's just dwell for a few moments on the deeper questions about life, because they affect how we approach our business and our personal lives.

If I ask: "How do you want your balance sheet to look

like at the end of your life?" How would you answer this question? Think about this for a moment...

Let me ask you an even more intense question. If you meet up with a group of strangers and someone asks you to tell them who you are, how would you answer that question? They then interrupt you when you start mentioning your job and location, saying they don't care about that. We want to know who you are.

This question is challenging because it asks you to let go of your material possessions and accomplishments. Someone asked me this question once, and I had to stop and think before I could answer this question. It felt like I was now my vulnerable self, stripped of things that I thought described myself.

Allowing myself to mull over the question made me realise that I am now confronted with the balance sheet of life, and not just a financial balance sheet. What does this mean? If I simply use the Biblical principle that we consist of body, soul, and spirit, then I have a relatively simple way to answer the questions of my balance sheet of life. I can compare my body with all the physical things in my life, like my work, business, and my finances. My soul can relate to how I manage relationships in my life, and my spirit can relate to my relationship with God.

Measuring my balance sheet of life in terms of those three dimensions helps me to create a balanced life. Therefore, to have a positive balance sheet at the end of my life I have to be bodily, emotionally, and spiritually fit.

We will elaborate on my bodily fitness later on in this chapter when I discuss what happened in my business. Let us reflect on what emotional and spiritual fitness mean.

We can compare our souls with relationships or emotional fitness. The test will then be how well we manage our relationships in our business and with family and friends.

Theodore Roosevelt rightly said: "People don't care how much you know until they know how much you care." This is true in both business and personal relationships. My clients certainly expect me to be competent in running their affairs, but they also want to know and experience that I truly care about them as people.

Stephen Covey has a wonderful way to explain this. He says relationships are like an emotional bank account or balance sheet. You make deposits and withdrawals. If you deposit more into your relationships than you withdraw then you will end up with a positive emotional balance sheet and vice versa. Deposits in relationships are things like keeping your promises and letting the client know that he received good value for the money spent. Withdrawals in relations are things like not keeping your promises or cheating your clients. The latter will eventually lead to a bankrupt emotional balance sheet.

Spiritual fitness will differ from person to person. We do not all believe in the same manner. Some people might perceive themselves to be a spiritual person even though they do not belong to a specific religion. Others might perceive their religion as the basis of their spiritual life. Different religions might share similar values. For instance, the value of stewardship is equally important in the Christian Bible, the Judaic Talmud, and Islam's Koran. They awarded the 14th Dalai Lama the Nobel Peace Prize for advocating peaceful solutions. He spoke words that resonate with most other religions. He said: "The purpose of life is to help others, and if you cannot help them, you should at least not hurt them."

My conviction of spiritual fitness is clear throughout this book. I am a child of God who believes Jesus Christ is my saviour. I learn from the wisdom that the Bible reveals and try to live by it. I share all my business decisions and other puzzling questions with God and listen to what His Spirit communicates to me.

Let us now return to my business life and what I had to do to move from a good business to a great business. Before I discuss the details of my business, I should mention that mentors on my path and my keen interest in learning made an impact on how I think and deal with business matters. I firmly believe that we should never stop learning and that we should associate with people from whom we can learn.

Andrew Carnegie was one of the most successful businesspersons in our history. They wrote his motto for a successful business on his tombstone. It reads: "Here lies one who knew how to get around him men who were cleverer than himself." This is real wisdom that I believe in. Wise business people will surround them with competent people.

The words, 'good to great,' is the title of a book written by Jim Collins. This book conveys wisdom and should be part of your essential reading list - particularly if you're a CEO looking to grow your business.

The 1st principle is that outstanding leaders will portray humility and strive to do the right thing for the good of the company, not themselves. This is true! The success of your company should be your driving force and not your personal gain.

The 2nd principle is the importance of 'getting the right people on the bus.' This resonated with the wisdom of Andrew Carnegie. *"It's not merely about filling positions but finding people with the desire to drive the company forward with you."* As a recruitment consultant, I understand this principle well.

His 3rd principle is that companies need to confront the brutal facts. It's about facing the future, armed with an unwavering resolve to face the facts, however stark they may be. I experienced this many times in my own business life!

The 4th principle is the Three Circles of The Hedgehog. The three elements are first, what you are passionate about. Then it is how you think you can make your company world-class and act upon it. Last is to understand the economic engine of your company and what generates your revenue. These three elements make absolute sense to me. I have seen how quickly we can get involved with activities that do not feed our bottom line and make us counterproductive.

His 5th principle is about the culture of your business. It is highly important to me. I know the importance of a winning culture and how difficult it is to maintain a winning culture in your business if you allow the wrong habits in your business. The culture in your business has a direct impact on the business strategy and eventual success of your company. It is best described by the words of Darryl Ackerman of Pick n Pay: "Culture eats strategy for breakfast."

The 6th principle is technology accelerators move companies from good to great. We should not underestimate the impact of this important principle. My son Michael plays a vital role in keeping us updated with the best technology.

The 7th principle is to create a flywheel that drives you to success. As I mentioned before, success breeds more success, just like a flywheel that starts rolling slowly but picks up speed. If everyone in the company understands their role and pushes toward the same goal, then the effect of the flywheel will become clear.

I trust you learned as much as I did from these seven principles. Let me now share what happened in my business. Let me just remind you again. I founded Directive Development Group (Pty) Ltd in 2012. I then reacted to an advert for a recruitment consultant to manage their company. They had only one client. I joined them as a service provider through Business Directive Development Group (Pty) Ltd, and not as an employee. I invoiced them.

When I started there, our monthly turnover was only R11 600. Then the sleeping giant within me woke up. Success has a way to breed more success. I experienced how total focus on a task can change small initial successes into a wave of successes that becomes larger and larger. When I left them in 2018, our turnover was over R8 million per month!

I was then approached to manage a contract for a leading South African online retailer. An opportunity arose in 2020 to purchase this contract. At that stage, 260 people were employed, and the turnover was approximately R34 million.

Business Directive Development Group (Pty) Ltd purchased the contract. We then created Business Directive Contract Services (Pty) Ltd to manage the contract. Business Directive Contract Services (Pty) Ltd functions as a separate entity but under Business Directive Development Group (Pty) Ltd.

Let me just give you some perspective on the challenges I faced when I bought this company. The outbreak of COVID-19 began in Wuhan, China, in December 2019. I decided to buy this contract at the beginning of the global pandemic and faced opposition from people who could not understand how I could take such a big step in the middle of a pandemic.

However, I was comfortable with my decision. It allowed me to think bigger, and I believed I could handle it. I took it on with full faith and worked hard to make my dream come true. I was not wrong. We started with a turnover of R34 million in 2020 and our expected turnover for this year is R231 million. Our staff grew from 260 people in 2020 to 2000 people.

Let me return to the words of Henry Ford at the beginning of this chapter: "Luck and destiny are the excuses for the world's failures." Was it luck and destiny that changed my business from good to great? I was lucky since online sales increased dramatically because of the movement restrictions during the COVID-19 pandemic. However, I did not know at the beginning of the COVID-19 pandemic that such dramatic restrictions would follow. My decision was based on the fact that I believed it was a good business decision and I had faith that I could make it work.

I believe that we create our own destinies by the way

we react to opportunities and threats. If you pursue the right opportunity and have the faith and tenacity to make it work, you create your own luck. Threats are also an opportunity to become more creative and to work smarter. You simply have to keep the faith!

On a practical note, I believe we do great because I surrounded myself with competent staff with a winning attitude. We do face challenges, make no mistake! However, if you create a winning culture in your business, you can overcome any challenge.

I believe in the principle of praise, rather than reprimand. Kenneth Blanchard and Spencer Johnson describe it in their book, The One Minute Manager. They teach us that leaders need to lead their staff to inner motivation.

Reprimand is if management just focuses on catching people out of what they do wrong. If this is the way the company manages its people, your staff will never become self-motivated.

However, if you focus on praising your staff by catching people out for what they do right, and you make sure they know it, they will become self-motivated to keep on doing great things. Therefore, we make sure that we celebrate successes to motivate our staff to do better.

I am closing this chapter here. The next chapter will be the last in this book. I will share some practical business and life lessons with you by using analogies from the Bible, nature, and some inspirational stories. Please join me on our journey to the final chapter…

TEN

The ancient wisdom of Indian chiefs regarding the dual wolves within us brings to mind the two perplexing wolves dwelling within us. I named them Fate and Destiny. "A fight is going on inside me. It is a terrible fight, and it is between Fate and Destiny. Fate believes my path is predetermined for me. Fate keeps me in prison to constantly wait for something to happen in the future. In the meantime, Fate allows other people and external circumstances to influence my life. The other wolf is Destiny. Destiny is restless and wants to act now. Destiny believes I make choices for myself to decide my future. This same fight is going on inside you and inside every other person, too."

The grandson asked his grandfather, "Which wolf will win?" The old chief replied, "The one you feed."

I choose to feed Destiny. Who do you choose to feed? In this final chapter, I want to share the importance of our inner person, and why we need to love ourselves and others. We are the sum of our experiences. It affects our mindsets which show up as our personality. Our mindset controls our outlook on our destiny. Negative thoughts lead to negative actions and vice versa. As a result, our daily life becomes simply a reflection of our inner programming.

I also want to share the importance of order in our lives and our businesses. Proper Governance became ever more important to ensure a sustainably profitable business. Analogies from nature and the wisdom from historical figures, such as Joseph will guide you throughout this chapter.

Destiny can often feel like fate in the idea that we are born on a specific date in a specific family in a specific place and that we will die on a predetermined date. I know that God decides the date of my birth and the date of my death, but God also gave me free will to decide what I do between those two dates.

It is often said that we cannot choose our family but we can choose our friends. However, how we relate to our family and act towards them is up to us, not some uncontrollable force.

Our choice of friends is also up to us. We can choose to have friends who share our joys and sorrows over our lifetime. There are some of our friends with whom we have a more intimate relationship than with some of our family. Friends are part of the family we choose.

My life is marked as the coat Joseph received from his father, one of many colours. I am blessed with true friends like Elbie and Magda and many other faithful friends. Friendships I formed over many years, each with its own dynamic and beauty. Lady friends such as Roline, with her beautiful smile and gentle nature, and Kallah, with whom I've tried out many exotic foods and enjoyed special moments just being a lady. Simone, who silently always looks out for me, encouraging me to rest and remember how precious I am. She makes any journey fun and exciting. I wish I could mention all of the colours in my coat, but trust you know who you are. You dress my soul when wounds are threatening to explode and leave me bare. Thank you for covering me with your love.

When people meet, they choose whether they want to be connected. You choose them and they choose you. It is not a predetermined relationship or forced connection. Family is more than just blood relatives. Friendships are life's way of showing us that family sometimes goes beyond a mere blood bond. Friends are family when you are freely connected. Love is the core of a relationship that brings happiness and support, not just blood.

Sibling rivalry started with the first two brothers in the history of mankind. The Lord looked with favour on Abel and his offering, but on Cain and his offering, he did not look with favour. From a human perspective, it seems unfair but God knows the motives of our hearts, our hidden agendas. Abel gave out of faith, and so he gave the best he had, entrusting himself to God. Cain gave without faith, not entrusting his best to God, who rewards those who seek Him.

Cain was angry because God did not accept him or his offer. Cain determined his destiny because he chose to become angry. He could have chosen to be regretful. Cain's choice to become angry then led to another choice.

He went along and killed his brother. Then the LORD said to Cain: "Where is your brother Abel?" Cain replied: "I don't know, Am I my brother's keeper?" Cain continues to choose wrongly, by lying.

Why am I sharing the story of Cain and Abel with you? To show you how the choices we make determine our destiny. Wrong choices can lead to more wrong choices. It creates a vicious cycle of disorder. God is righteous and likes order. If we follow His wisdom, we will create order in our lives and our businesses. We are the consequences of our choices.

Nature was created before man. Nature is an example of order and therefore part of the Creator's character and preference. If one spends time in nature, you soon realise how diverse and organised nature is. It is a remarkable, self-regulating ecosystem of synergy amidst diversity and uniqueness. Everything in nature, from the macrocosm of the galaxies to the microcosm of the atom and cells, was put together with remarkable thoroughness. No element of the macro or microcosm is neglected - and this applies to all living beings from man to animals and plants.

Nature can create order out of disorder. Seasoned business leaders can also make a business thrive through mistakes by replacing disorder with order-creating decisions. Of course, it takes energy to create order out of chaos and maintain it. The Creator turned the disorder of the universe into an orderly system, which is held in balance by conflicting forces. The business world is also a cosmos of constant challenges, increasing competition, and conflicting interests, in an ever-changing global marketplace. It requires energy to survive in this business battlefield.

However, the natural world is also oriented towards harmony. It naturally changes to restore any imbalance in nature. This law of nature offers businessmen numerous life and moral lessons. Elephants teach us, for example, the importance of experience in that the oldest female with the most experience leads the herd. Elephants also show us the importance of cooperation when different elephant herds in difficult times work together to survive. Businesses must also tap into the experience of employees and in difficult times, different enterprises must stand together to protect their industry. We saw how businesses stood together during the COVID-19 pandemic to protect their industry.

The bat-eared fox teaches us the importance of early warning systems when he uses his nearest neighbour, the meerkat with its keen eyesight, to know when danger is approaching. Businesses also need early warning systems, such as the regular testing of gross and net profit margins, so they can respond in time to avoid cash flow problems.

The Bible refers to the lessons that we can learn from four small, but wise, animals. For example, ants gather their food supply in the summer to survive the coming winter. In the same way, we must learn in our enterprises to not deplete all our profits in times of great returns but to save for the "winter months" that our company may experience.

Our Creator created mankind in His image. He is a creator and if we are created in His image then we can be creative, or be entrepreneurial, in a business sense. The term "entrepreneur" originated from the French word *entreprendre* meaning "to undertake." That is what business leaders do daily. We take on the responsibility of managing our businesses.

People often speculate about whether successful entrepreneurs are born or bred. Do entrepreneurs have a natural talent for business, or can this be developed? It probably helps if you are born into a family-owned business and therefore grow up in a business environment. I did not grow up in such an environment and had to learn through trial and error.

A hunting leopard pauses instantly when it sees a

potential prey. Through learning, the leopard knows how the specific prey will react when hunted and will plan his attack accordingly. Entrepreneurs also learn through trial and error how to sharpen their business-hunting skills. Animals who hunt in a pack, such as the wild dogs of Africa, will act as a team to ensure success. In the same way, teamwork is vital for business success.

Each of us carries around an image of ourselves in our minds. The image may be vague or clear and to a greater or lesser extent differ from how others see us. The image we have of ourselves, namely our self-image, is built up from the conceptions we have of ourselves. We are what we think. Our thoughts control our actions. The late Louis Malherbe, a life coach and author of books such as Maximum Man and Maximum Mates, has always quoted an old wisdom: You are not who you think you are, but what you think, that you are. Yes, the way we think determines who we are and what our perspectives are.

We need to appreciate who we are and how unique we were created. The late Professor Leo Buscaglia said that he often asks seminar participants whom they would most like to be. The shocking answer is that more than eighty percent of all the people answering the question, want to be someone other than themselves. What a tragedy! The largest percentage of mankind wants to be someone else!

You are all you have and must make the most of yourself.

To value ourselves we must make an effort to know ourselves and our good and bad qualities. Second, we must learn to accept our unique selves, because only then can you give yourself to others and love yourself. If you believe the words: *You must love your neighbour as yourself*, you are going to struggle to love others if you don't even accept and love yourself!

Success is often measured by achievements and material things rather than the inner side of each person. We look with conditioned eyes and do not see the unique wealth within ourselves and others. Our dear Father looked at Adam and saw in him a world full of people and in Abraham, he saw nations. In David, he saw a king, not a mere shepherd.

There is an ancient law that will always remain in force, a law that is thousands of years old and recorded in the Bible: "What you sow, you will reap."

Joseph, a well-known character in the Old Testament, is an example of someone who lived the sowing and reaping principle. His brothers threw him into a well; he was sold into slavery by the same brothers, wrongfully convicted of adultery with his employer's wife, and finally thrown into prison. However, Joseph remained positive, persisted in his faith, and was eventually appointed by the Pharaoh as second in command of Egypt. He also forgave his brothers and they carried him on their hands after that.

The story of Joseph is an excellent analogy to teach us how to deal with the trials and tribulations we may experience during our lifetime in our personal lives and businesses. It also teaches us great leadership lessons.

As you know by now, my life was not smooth sailing. It was a life-changing moment when I experienced a moment of self-pity and my son Michael told me: "Mom, many people smoke, drink alcohol, or use drugs to cope with the adversities of life. You have God! Ask Him to make you stronger!"

This was a wake-up moment in 2012 and became a life skill I still apply whenever I'm tempted to let life's difficulties get me down. I ask God to make me stronger! I have made mistakes and faced adversity. It is how I dealt with adversity that determined my destiny. The Lord tried and tested me to see if I keep my faith. The reason why

Life was certainly not just smooth sailing for Joseph. The description of what Joseph had to face in Psalm 105: verses 7 to 9 (Amplified Bible: Classic Edition) resonates with my own life and the title of this book, Iron in Silk, as André described me in the Prologue of this book. Joseph was sold as a servant and jailed. *His feet, hurt with fetters; he was laid in chains of iron and his soul entered into the iron, until his word [to his cruel brothers] came true, until the word of the Lord tried and tested him.*

Joseph dreamt about his future as I did since childhood. I knew God had a plan for my life but did not know what it was. The many trials and tribulations during my life did not silence my dream. Joseph's life depicts a sense of order and sound governance. I will explore the importance of this later on.

The words, *his soul entered into the iron*, have a very deep meaning. For iron to enter your soul sounds painful and it is. But it is precisely painful experiences that sharpen your wisdom and eventually delight your soul. God has set up Joseph's life through trials and tribulations to prepare him to rule and reign as a leader only second to Pharoah.

Joseph was criticised by his brothers. They hated him because he believed in his dreams, and his destiny, and did not hesitate to speak about it. They spoke evil about him. As I evolve in my business life, I also experience people who try to disparage me. Nothing tests our character more than having something evil said about us. The kind of grinding test is what exposes whether we are solid iron or simply plated metal. If we could only see the blessings that lie hidden in our trials, we would say like David, when he was cursed, let him curse me. It may be that the LORD will repay me with good for the cursing I am receiving today.

Let us focus on the essence of good leadership that we can learn from Joseph. **Joseph was a servant leader.** The term servant leadership is an integral part of Biblical wisdom. It makes me involuntarily think of Jesus' words in Mark 9:35: "If anyone wants to be first, let him be the very last and the servant of all." In a business context this also means that if you want to be first in the business world, you must learn to be a servant. We must first learn to serve our business before we can reap the benefits of our business.

The general concept of serving as a leader comes from the ancient time. Chanakya in the fourth century B.C. in his book Arthashastra wrote: "The king (leader) is a paid servant who enjoys the resources of the state together with his people and must therefore do what is good for the people and not what is good for himself.

The concept of Servant Leadership was introduced in our modern times in 1970 by Robert K. Greenleaf. It began when he referred to "the servant as leader" and other terms such as "servant-leader" and used "servant leadership". He defines the servant leader as follows: "The servant-leader is servant first. It starts with the natural feeling that one wants to serve, to serve first." From a business point of view, it means that we will create great business results if we truly serve our customers.

Joseph remained patient through the bad times. Joseph went through many hardships but he faithfully and patiently waited to realise his dream. Nowadays we hear more and more how preachers promote the so-called *prosperity theology*. It is the popular belief that those who love God, think positively, and work hard will receive material wealth and success. The story of Joseph stands in stark opposition to this. Joseph did everything right, and still spent thirteen years as a slave or prisoner.

Let me just emphasise an important Biblical lesson. If your sole purpose in business is money, and that becomes your only desire, then I need to warn you about the wisdom we found in 1 Timothy 6:10: *For the love of money is a root of all evils, by means of which some having lusted after it were seduced from the faith, and they pierced through by many pains.*

Be careful that money does not become your god. Yes, we are in business to turn a profit, and rightly so. However, our first focus should be to serve our clients well, and if we do, profits will follow. Just remember to be patient and keep on doing the right things and you will eventually reap the benefits. Rome was not built in a day is an idiom that we should take note of. The true meaning is that nothing great comes without hard work, time dedication, and patience.

Joseph had to learn humility to be a good leader. God allowed Joseph to be a slave and a prisoner to teach him humility. Humble leaders aren't afraid to make mistakes. We all make mistakes. That is how we learn. Humility leads to the inner drive to learn to become better at what you do.

Humble leaders deal with the profound changes in the business world because they are willing to never stop learning. I love the way Al Rogers describes this: *"In times of profound change, the learners inherit the earth, while the learned find themselves beautifully equipped to deal with a world that no longer exists."*

Humble leaders listen better. There is a reason why we are born with one mouth and two ears. Leaders who listen well don't realise how popular they are! Leaders must learn the art of dynamically listening to staff and consumers. A dynamic listener is actively involved in a conversation; he constantly listens, interprets, and responds.

Humility in the workplace can encourage your staff to also go out of their way to help others, which results in a more productive business.

Joseph was caring and showed emotion. Joseph wept when he saw his brothers in Egypt after many years. Faced with the family members who betrayed him, Joseph displayed compassion, forgiveness, and love. Some leaders believe they should not show emotion, but they are wrong. Leaders who openly show emotion show that they are a caring, loving leader.

These leadership lessons of Joseph are dear to me and encourage me to act in the same manner. Though we may not be called to lead a nation like Joseph, God calls all of us to lead in some way. Whether we manage our business or serve our community, Joseph's life as a leader provides us with a framework to effectively serve as leaders.

I will now borrow some analogies from nature from Andre's books to further explain what great leadership means to me. One of the most remarkable trees is the olive tree. It reflects leadership naturally. In South Africa, this tree is not common in every household. In the Middle-East, and countries around the Mediterranean, olives have been around for thousands of years as a source of food. Its oil is also used for cooking purposes and to light lamps to provide light. It is also used for anointing and religious ceremonies. In Israel, this tree stands everywhere on the mountain slopes of Galilee, Judea, and Samaria.

Just looking at an olive tree brings a sense of wisdom and strength because this tree has managed to survive for thousands of years in the worst cold and heat with minimum water. It can also survive in too much water because it was a freshly picked olive leaf that a dove brought to Noah's ark to indicate that the water had begun to recede. No matter what was swallowed up by the flood waters, the olive tree was still alive!

Even if the tree is burned to the ground, it will simply just grow again. The tree has character, the kind of character that leads to long-term survival, the same kind of character traits that help ethical business leaders to make businesses survive in the long term. The oldest family business in the world is Congo Gumi, a Japanese temple builder, who started in AD 578 and is currently in its fiftieth generation. What olive tree lessons can't we learn from them?

Like the olive tree continues to bear fruit, we as leaders must also, regardless of our life circumstances, remain steadfast and, like the olive tree, always bear the right fruit. Through this steadfast action, we will instil our values in our followers and thus multiply them, just as there are ten or more new shoots all around the olive tree that grows from its root system.

Leadership offers the potential to empower others and to share in the returns that the company produces. Empowerment involuntarily reminds me of the analogy of the olive tree that Paul uses in Romans 11:17 to illustrate empowerment. The natural branch in this analogy is the nation of Israel. Christians are the branches grafted between the natural branches and share the root and the greasiness of the olive tree.

It is evident from the Bible passage, and also from nature, that the root and the trunk bear the branches, just as the company and its leadership carry the employees. The employees must therefore respect the root (enterprise) that provides the work and the employer must empower the employee to do a good job to enable the leaders and its employees to share in the fruit.

Leadership and values are two sides of the same coin. The values that leaders illustrate will directly impact how their followers perceive and experience them. Ethical values will strengthen your leadership.

To better understand the connection between leadership and values, we can look at the relationship between the olive tree and essential oils. A base oil, or carrier oil, is normally mixed with essential oils because it is too strong to use clean. In our analogy, olive oil, derived from the olive tree, is the base oil and it embodies leadership. The essential oils with the base oil, are the values that leadership supports.

Imagine a bowl of olive oil and a hand that pours essential oils into the olive oil. These essential oils can be jasmine, rose, or many others depending on our needs and preferences. Every essential oil represents a specific value. By mixing the essential oils (values) with the olive oil as a base oil (leadership), we then obtain a result that we can take advantage of.

I now want to focus on the importance of good governance. Let us return to Joseph. A core value that Joseph clearly illustrated was corporate citizenship. He loved order and hated lawlessness in the same manner that Jesus loved righteousness and hated lawlessness (Hebrews 1 verse 9). In today's terms, we refer to this as governance.

Let us just pause for a moment and reflect on the importance of corporate citizenship. Our company has just been nominated in the category of corporate citizenship. I feel as strongly as Joseph about proper governance and corporate citizenship.

The Josephson Institute did an extensive research project with 133,000 respondents from all ethnic and religions to determine universal values that everyone believes in. These values became the Six Pillars of Character– trustworthiness, respect, responsibility, fairness, caring and corporate citizenship. They describe corporate citizenship as *Honour and respect the principles and spirit of democracy and set a positive example by observing the letter and spirit of laws.* They promote that you should play by the rules and obey laws.

Globalisation has increased the focus on governance. The world is becoming a common marketplace and investors are investing more and more in global markets. This poses a challenge to the world because business regulation, or governance, differs from country to country. It places the focus on global governance, which implies the world will have to agree on global rules.

It impacts governments and companies alike since the legislation in countries affects the application of governance by the governments and companies, hence the focus on public and corporate governance.

In terms of corporate governance, two conflicting theories evolved in the world, the so-called shareholders' theory and the stakeholder's theory. Milton Friedman is known for the shareholder theory and stated in his famous article in the New York Times: "The social responsibility of business is to increase its profits." He denies that business has any social responsibilities other than making a profit. As Friedman's name is associated with the shareholder theory, so is Edward Freeman associated with the stakeholder theory. Drawing from a legal argument, Freeman states that different stakeholders of corporations, such as employees, suppliers, and customers, have rights that need to be respected.

The stakeholder theory won the global battle and all participating countries had to adapt their governance regulation. South Africa's reaction is worth mentioning since the King's reports emphasised the essence of governance in the world today. The King 1 report incorporates a Code of Corporate Practices and Conduct. This was an integrated approach, which included the interests of a wide range of stakeholders. King 11 moved drastically away from a single bottom line approach (profit for shareholders) to a triple bottom line approach. The triple-bottom-line approach includes economic, environmental, and socio-ethical bottom lines. This is in line with the general sentiment in the world today.

To comply with global governance and the King reports, South Africa had to update its business regulations. This led to the New Consumer Protection Act and the New Regulations of the Company's Act that came into force on 1 April 2011.

It is very clear to me that ethics, or business ethics, are driving the governance regulation in the world today. They want to enforce ethical business practices through regulation. For me, it is a pity that we need regulation to force ethical business practices but I understand why it is needed. Ethics is a necessity for me because it is my conviction.

The subject of ethics has been addressed since biblical times and philosophers such as Socrates and Aristotle all shaped the thinking in the world. The ethics of business has been addressed as far back as in the Old Testament of God's Word.

The Jews, for example, attended to moral issues in business during biblical times by teaching their followers that, when reaping the wheat harvest, they must leave enough behind to feed the poor. The Classic Greeks, the originators of modern civilisation, also attended to moral values in the business environment.

Ethics is derived from the Greek word *ethos*, meaning *character*, while morality is derived from the Latin word *mores*, meaning *custom*. Aristotle defines virtue as an activity of the soul.

How people act towards themselves and others is the field of study called *ethics*. Another name for *ethics* is *morality*. Sometimes people make a distinction between ethics and morality. However, most people do not. Ethics and morals are used interchangeably. Behaviour can be acceptable or unacceptable, right or wrong, ethical or unethical.

Ethics is a matter of choice, but this choice has changed into a regulated choice. I am not convinced that regulation will automatically let all people behave ethically and that people should voluntarily behave ethically, but let me leave it there.

Corporate governance brings us closer to the subject of business ethics. Business plays an integral part in the way the global environment is evolving and governed. If one keeps in mind that the 100 largest economies in the world include 51 companies, the impact of business becomes clear.

Business ethics refers to the principles, norms, and standards that an organisation promotes for the guidance and conduct of its activities, internal relationships, and interactions with external stakeholders. An organisation should ensure that measurement, monitoring, and review processes exist to ensure the application of ethical standards.

Professor Deon Rossouw states: "It resolves around three central concepts: self, good, and other. Each of these three central concepts must be included in a definition of ethics. Should the concept of good be neglected, the unique nature of ethics collapses."

I do not wish to elaborate on the academic description

of ethics and choose to stick to the simplest definition of ethics, namely the ability to choose between right and wrong.

Choices between right and wrong are based on what an individual or society believes to be right and wrong. The concept of what is right or wrong is based on an individual or society's value system. Some find criteria in Christianity, Islam, or some other religion, while others let history lead them.

The Bible is my reference to good morals or ethical values. Ethics focus on human character, while Christian ethics is rooted in God's character. There will be similarities between human ethics and Christian ethics, as there are similarities between Christian ethics, and ethics of most other religions, e.g., Hinduism, Buddhism, and Islam. Human ethics is flawed, as people in different time frames seek new meanings to cope with a changing world. God's ethics as prescribed in His Holy Word is flawless and never changes.

I want to end the discussion about ethics and governance by reminding you of what I said earlier in this chapter. God is righteous and likes order. If we follow His wisdom, we will create order in our lives and our businesses. I want to state categorically that I believe and practice good governance because it ensures good order. In my experience, it is the only way to create a sustainably profitable business. Therefore, I make sure that we follow clear guidelines in my business to ensure order and good conduct.

I want to end this chapter with lessons I learned in André's book about leadership values. He says, that our outlook on ethics will be influenced by our value system. I fully agree, it is certainly our values that determine what we perceive as ethical. I will add my comments to his wisdom.

The departure of his Afrikaans book, loosely translated as *Leadership Values: Wisdom from the Plant Kingdom*, is that the average lifespan of businesses in the world is 24 years. He wanted to know the reason why some businesses have been around for centuries and even longer than a millennium. He communicated with the oldest businesses in the world to find an answer.

The answer from all these businesses was consistently that they survived for so long because of their values. Values that they instilled amongst their children and employees from generation to generation as the way they do things and it is non-negotiable.

He then asked them what these values are and completed the book about the values most of the oldest businesses instilled and compared these values with trees and plants. These values are powerful if you apply them consistently.

The first value is consistency. Values are only truly of value if applied consistently. Consistency is therefore the foundation of all other values and therefore the first value discussed in this book. Just as the day can only dawn when the sun rises and the night only when the sun gives way to the moon and stars, each value will only ensure the sustainability of your business if the values are consistently applied.

Consistency builds self-esteem because you stay faithful to your principles and fundamental nature. Others will respect you if they see that you show a strong character by standing up for what you believe in and what you value.

The second value is fairness. Fairness must be learned like many other important life lessons. Certain lessons are fast and easily learned, such as that your hand will burn if you touch a hot stovetop. Other lessons can be much longer and expensive and sometimes even take a lifetime before it is learned and applied.

Fairness is probably one of the most difficult values to apply consistently because man by nature puts his interest first. To be fair requires a heart that cares for others. A leader who can find the balance between his own needs and the needs of others applies the greatest command, namely to love others as oneself.

There is nothing that can make people more dissatisfied than being treated unfairly. It is the undertone of almost all revolutions that we have experienced in the world and also in our own country. In our businesses, fairness includes several other underlying values, such as equality and impartiality. Be careful, or your employees will revolt against unfairness and favouritism.

The third value is vision. I remember well how I as a child, like many other children, could dream about who and what I would be one day and of all the incredible things I envisioned. I could sit and daydream for hours and I still do!

A dream in the business world and the world of leadership has another name. We call it a vision. Vision is a mental picture, like a dream, of how you want your future to be like.

A leader without a vision of the future is like a blind man in a strange place that feels forward to the unknown. I would go so far as to say that vision is a prerequisite for successful leadership. Followers who understand your vision find it easier to follow you.

It's also important to give your people the feeling that they are involved in a vision. It encourages them and makes them feel like they are playing an important part in the bigger picture. A good analogy to lead people to become more, is when Jesus said to the fishermen: "Follow me, I will make you fishers of men." That same "wow" feeling that these simple fishermen at that moment must have experienced, is what followers need to help you to realise your vision.

The fourth value is servant leadership. I discussed this before in detail. I would just like to add something else. Servant leadership is an every-moment-of-every-day action. John Wesley's words illustrate this well "Do what you can, as well as you can, wherever you can, for as long as you can."

The fifth value is integrity. Integrity does not simply mean to believe in moral and ethical principles, but indeed to live and maintain these principles at all times. There is no such thing as "grades of integrity." You either have integrity or you don't. It is like theft, whether you steal R1 or R1 000 000, does not change the fact that you stole.

Leaders with integrity can have many enemies. To completely live a life of integrity can leave a leader lonely, but at the same time offers inner peace; something money or power cannot buy. Abraham Lincoln was known as, "Honest Abe." Abe chose to make integrity his best friend. In his own words: "When I down the reins of this administration, I want to have one friend left, and that friend (my integrity) shall be inside myself."

John Maxwell clearly illustrated the personal nature of integrity when a well-known publisher asked him to write a book about business ethics. He became silent and said that he unfortunately could not write such a book. The publisher wanted to know why not. To the publisher's surprise, John said that there is no such thing as business ethics because ethics (or integrity) is a personal value and cannot take shape in a company if it is not first of all a personal value!

I love the way André compares integrity with Jasmine. Jasmine undergoes a chemical change during sunset in that the aroma intensifies as the darkness approaches. It is, therefore, the best time to pluck it. Integrity's biggest test is who we are when no one is looking or when problems and difficult circumstances make it dark around us.

The scent of jasmine cannot be matched with any other scent. It's unmistakably jasmine. Let the people around enjoy the pure scent of your integrity, just as jasmine can soothe our senses.

The sixth value is empowerment. True leaders can see the possibility in people and unlock it. Richard Branson is an example of a contemporary business leader who unlocks the potential of people with great success. Most organisations' philosophy is that the customer is king and must be served at all costs. This is a good philosophy, but should not be at the expense of your employees. Branson believes that your employees should be your main focus and not your customers BECAUSE happy employees will result in happy customers and unhappy employees result in unhappy customers! Richard's business results speak for itself.

The art of leadership is to create leaders. That's the true test of leadership! Just like a clean sheet of paper and a brush in the hand of a talented artist can become a work of art, people can in the hands of a talented leader become a masterpiece.

Jesus is an example of a leader who was eager to develop others who could take over from Him. He didn't stop there. He told his followers that they would do greater things than Himself. Jesus did not look down on his followers and never tried to protect his leadership position No, He constantly encouraged others to take the lead and do bigger things than Himself. Thomas Carlyle's words are also wise: "A great man shares his greatness by the way he treats little men."

The seventh value is wisdom. The increasing emphasis on knowledge, or intellectual capital, in the Information and Communication Revolution in which we live, has caused wisdom to enjoy less attention. Knowledge is very important, but wisdom is vital for effective leadership.

It is the application of knowledge with integrity that brings us closer to wisdom. For leaders, wisdom is also the ability to make and carry out choices to deliver the optimum results in the minimum time with the minimum energy. To be clever or have knowledge is good, but wisdom teaches us to work smart. Wisdom comes with experience. It's experiences that teach us to find and follow the right path. C.J Langenhoven wisely said: "The smart man knows all the paths, the wise know the one right path."

The father of wisdom is King Solomon. His proverbs are meant to teach people wisdom. Even wise people can listen to these proverbs and thus come to a deeper insight. Wisdom is indeed to constantly seek for deeper insights. The book of Solomon, Proverbs, states that wisdom begins with serving the Lord. For reference see Psalm 111:10, Proverbs 1:7, and 9:10.

The eighth value is passion. Leadership is passion! Without it, you will have little positive influence on others. Your passion as a leader causes others to imitate you. Passion unlocks energy. A definition of passion that sticks with me is: "Leaders are people who leave footprints in their areas of passion" (anon).

The passion that feeds leadership can be positive or negative. Unfortunately, we can passionately do the wrong things! Like gambling or drinking too much. Hitler was extremely passionate. Unfortunately, it was not a positive purpose and led to the death of six million of our Jewish brothers and sisters in unimaginable circumstances. Passion must therefore be ethical.

The passion in every leader is as strong as the fire that is burning inside! Passionate devotion to what you believe in will spread like wildfire among your followers. Passion requires the courage of your conviction. Warren Bennis says: "Good leaders make people feel that they're at the very heart of things, not at the periphery. Everyone feels that he or she makes a difference in the success of the organisation. When that happens, people feel centered and that gives their work meaning." True passion is contagious!

The last value I want to discuss is stewardship. Stewards do the right things today to create a better tomorrow. Stewards, or custodians, are servant leaders and servant leaders are stewards. It is stewardship that sustains businesses over generations. Leaders who are stewards want to leave a lasting legacy, as an example for others. They treat their own company's resources with respect.

Stewardship is like the cedar tree. Cedar trees reflect strength and endurance and are considered indestructible for millennia. King Solomon was wise enough to build the temple with cedar wood because he knew that cedar wood was incorruptible. We can still see the cedar trees with which King Solomon's temple was built, on Mount Lebanon as a symbol of incorruptibility. A symbol of stewardship.

Concluding remarks:
Thank you for allowing me to share my journey with you. Success is only sweet if it is significant and it can only be significant if your success empowers others to be successful.

The purpose of life is neither about you or me, nor about personal fulfilment, but about the contribution we can make to others. The great musician Pablo Casales said: "Each person has a basic decency and goodness inside themselves. If he acts on it and listens to it, he is giving a great deal of what the world needs most. It is not complicated but it takes courage. It takes courage for a person to listen to his own goodness and act upon it."

The poet William Wordsworth put it another way, declaring that the best portion of a good person's life is "little, nameless, unremembered acts of kindness and love." The novelist Henry James said: "Three things in human life are important: The first is to be kind. The second is to be kind. And the third is to be kind."

Our legacy will only be lasting if it does not conflict with God's wisdom. **God doesn't guard what He doesn't build.** True greatness is measured in Godly character, wisdom, self-control, patience, love, service, and purity. Let us think about the impact of our decisions. Let us find a balance between personal gain (or profit) and people. Be kind to others.

Live and practice the words of Philippians 2:4 (GW) *"Don't be concerned only about your own interests, but also be concerned about the interests of others."* Let us not forget:

I AM BECAUSE YOU ARE!

BIBLIOGRAPHY

Books
Bible, several translations
Diederichs, AW 2007. *People versus Profit.* Kaapstad: People versus Profit Movement.
Diederichs, AW. 2008. *Business Jungle.* Kaapstad: Naledi.
Diederichs, AW. 2009. *Veldwysheid.* Kaapstad: Naledi.
Diederichs, AW. 2010. *Leierskapswaardes: Wysheid uit die planteryk.* Kaapstad: Naledi.
Diederichs, AW. 2014. *Bemark of Bevark.* Kaapstad: Naledi.
Diederichs, AW. 2022. Nalatenskap. Kaapstad: Naledi.

Radio
Diederichs, AW. 2015 – 2023. Cape Pulpit & Radio Namakwaland

Websites:
https://leadersgolast.com/the-story-of-joseph-in-the-bible-the-patient-leader/
https://www.bsfblog.org/leadership-lessons-from-joseph/

Miskyah, Owner, Sole Shareholder and Director of Business Directive Development Group (Pty) Ltd. BDCS, a dynamic, fast-growing Temporary Employ-ment Agency, nominated for Corporate Citizenship is part of this dynamic group.

She runs her profit organisations with an iron fist, while her heart bursts forth as the lady in silk in her long-standing non-profit endeavours in Miskyah.com. Miskyah has won international awards for her business acumen as well as her resilience to never give up, regardless of any resistance. She completed a BA Degree at the University of Pretoria in 1986. She resumed her studies many years later to complete an Honours Laureate in Theology, with Distinction in 2021. Her dissertation for this study focused on success principles found in the Jewish culture as indicators for success in business and communities.

She raised two successful sons as a divorced mother and experienced lack in ways many don't, but this became the fuel for her firm belief that success and wealth are determined by our own decisions and that it's worth fighting for. She defeated lack and is now a multi-millionaire with wisdom and a style of Business Management that speaks to good governance and the gem of enjoying the thrill of overcoming obstacles.

She has recently been nominated as Top Business Woman

in South Africa by a leading financial institution and at the time of the publishing of this book, awaited the result.

She spent many years on her 'golf' field in studios as a Radio Presenter for different stations. This way she served communities and rubbed shoulders with phenomenal business people.

She subscribed to a healthy lifestyle and qualified as an Advanced Scuba Diver after the age of 50. Travelling the world and enjoying the beauty of diverse cultures and histories are the things this lady treasures. A highlight for her was the freedom of floating high above the earth in a hot air balloon in Cappadocia, Turkey.

Her motto: Life is a dance; we only need to tune our ears to the song and then dance as if this moment is the only important one!

www.ingramcontent.com/pod-product-compliance
Lightning Source LLC
Chambersburg PA
CBHW020858160426
43192CB00007B/973